COPYRIGHT & LAW FOR WRITERS

Other How To Books on Successful Writing

Copyright & Law for Writers
Creating a Twist in the Tale
Creative Writing
How to Be a Freelance Journalist
How to Master Business English
How to Publish a Book
How to Publish a Newsletter
How to Start Word Processing
How to Write a Press Release
How to Write a Report
How to Write an Assignment
How to Write an Essay
How to Write & Sell Computer Software
How to Write Business Letters
How to Write for Publication
How to Write for Television
How to Write Your Dissertation
Starting to Write
Writing a Non-fiction Book
Writing Reviews
Writing & Selling a Novel
Writing & Selling Short Stories

Other titles in preparation

The How To series now contains more than 150 titles in the following categories:

Business Basics
Family Reference
Jobs & Careers
Living & Working Abroad
Student Handbooks
Successful Writing

Please send for a free copy of the latest catalogue for full details (see back cover for address).

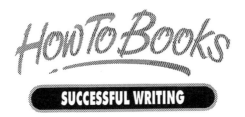

SUCCESSFUL WRITING

COPYRIGHT & LAW FOR WRITERS

How to protect yourself and your creative work

Helen Shay

AND DON'T LET ME CATCH YOU PHOTOCOPYING IT ALL ...

LIBRARY

LAW

How To

By the same author in this Series:

Making a Complaint: How to put your case successfully and win redress

Cartoons by Mike Flanagan

British Library Cataloguing-in-publication data
A catalogue record for this book is available from the British Library.

First published in 1996 by How To Books Ltd, Plymbridge House, Estover Road, Plymouth PL6 7PZ, United Kingdom. Tel: Plymouth (01752) 202301. Fax: (01752) 202331.

Note: The material contained in this book is set out in good faith for general guidance only and no liability can be accepted for loss or expense incurred as a result of relying in particular circumstances on statements made in the book. The law and regulations are complex and liable to change, and readers should check the current position with the relevant authorities before making personal arrangements.

Produced for How To Books by Deer Park Productions.
Typeset by PDQ Typesetting, Stoke-on-Trent, Staffs.
Printed and bound by The Cromwell Press, Broughton Gifford, Melksham, Wiltshire.

Contents

List of illustrations 8

Foreword 9

1 **What use are your rights?** 11

How important is the law to you as a writer? 11
Is the law an ass? 12
Watching out for legal dangers 12
Gaining the rewards of knowing your rights 13
Case studies – introduction 14
Summary 15
Discussion points 15

2 **Using your copyright** 16

What is copyright? 16
Knowing your 'moral rights' 21
Preserving these rights 23
Avoiding infringement of copyright 24
Case studies 24
Summary 26
Discussion points 27

3 **Utilising material** 28

Inputting sources within your text 28
How much can you quote? 29
Acknowledging your sources 31
Avoiding plagiarism 31
Photocopying 34
Understanding data protection 34
Case studies 35
Summary 36
Discussion points 37

4   **Avoiding libel**   38

    What is libel?   38
    How far can you go?   39
    Preventing legal action   40
    Defending legal action   42
    Case studies   43
    Summary   45
    Discussion points   45

5   **Entering a contract**   46

    Understanding basic contract law   46
    Do you need an agent?   48
    Insisting on the essentials   50
    Amending the small print   54
    Case studies   55
    Summary   57
    Discussion points   58

6   **Getting out of a contract**   59

    What if it all goes wrong?   59
    When is a contract not a contract?   59
    How can I end my contract?   60
    Using a termination clause   63
    Getting redress   63
    Case studies   64
    Summary   66
    Discussion points   66

7   **Getting paid**   68

    Taking 'persuasive' measures   68
    Deciding to sue   70
    Using the small claims court   71
    Claiming for larger amounts   72
    Reaching a settlement   73
    Case studies   73
    Summary   75
    Action points   75

8   **Sorting out other problems**   76

9   **Appreciating legal aspects of self-publishing**   78

    Is it for you?   78
    Choosing the type of organisation   78
    Forming a company or club   79
    Choosing a name   81
    Dealing with other formalities   81
    Case studies   83
    Summary   84
    Discussion points   85

10 **Dealing with your literary estate**   86

    Making a will   86
    Choosing the right executors   86
    Planning for the future   87
    Tax   87
    Case studies   87
    Summary   88
    Discussion points   88

Glossary   89

Useful addresses   91

Further reading   93

Index   94

List of Illustrations

1. Copyright notice 19

2. Table of rights 20

3. Sample clause relating to general sources 31

4. Table of sample contract clauses 56

5. Sample termination clause 62

6. Letter before action 70

7. Sample particulars of claim 72

8. Sample extract of a memorandum of association including the main objects clause 80

Foreword

In a long career as a writer I've seen hard times come and then go. But the present hard times may be, like King Charles, an unconscionable time a-dying.

After abandonment of the Net Book Agreement, publishers are murmuring they want to renegotiate contracts; newspaper chains have been trying to grab all the electronic rights in articles submitted to them; magazines seem less willing to take freelance work and if they do, delay payment; TV production companies impose very severe rules about looking at a new author's work; and a new, and cleverer, race of vanity publishers seems ready to trick an inexperienced poet or book author.

Our writing world is changing very fast and not, it seems, to our advantage. It is vital not to let ourselves be exploited or diminished in face of new technology and new circumstances. We may find we need to assert ourselves, to insist on our rights.

You ask: What are my rights? Simply *knowing a few facts* is often enough to reduce a troublesome editor or publisher to order.

With this book, you have in Helen Shay a source of help at hand at all times – from someone who cares about writers!

Jean Bowden
Vice-President and Past Chairman of the
Society of Women Writers and Journalists,
Past Chairman of the Crime Writers Association.
As Tessa Barclay, author of many novels
published by Headline Books

IS THIS YOU?

Writer   Journalist

                    Author

Researcher   Student

                  Biographer

Feature writer   Illustrator

                  Book editor

Newsletter publisher   Agent

                 Photographer

Designer   Poet

                Memoirs writer

Short story writer   Novelist

                 Writing tutor

Essayist   Lawyer

                  Interviewer

Broadcaster   Bookseller

                Magazine editor

Scriptwriter   Caption writer

                  Script editor

Radio producer   Television producer

                Book distributor

Copy editor   Sub editor

                   Freelance

Dramatist   Self-publisher

                 Travel writer

1
What Use Are Your Rights?

If a man knows the law, there is nothing he cannot do when he likes.
(*Vera*, Oscar Wilde)

HOW IMPORTANT IS THE LAW TO YOU AS A WRITER?

This book aims to help you, the writer, to:

- enjoy your full rights
- avoid legal pitfalls
- eliminate any come-back upon you.

It may be particularly useful to 'up and coming' writers. They cannot yet command 'the clout' of the bestsellers and often find that their lack of bargaining power in the present publishing climate is a threat to a fulfilling career.

Writing and the law have much in common. Words are their mutual stock-in-trade. Both aim to use these to a precise effect: the one to engage the reader; the other to define (or bend) the rules within which society operates. Because of this, you as a writer are especially equipped to understand the subtleties of the law. And so you should. It affects your working life, whether you recognise it or not:

- during the writing process itself
- in approaches and negotiations for publication
- on publication and thereafter.

The law is of great significance to you as a writer. Knowledge of it is power.

Main areas of law helpful to a writer
Copyright: which gives you the author control over your work. It cannot be copied, published, produced or adapted without your agreement.

Moral rights: which are attached to copyright and give you the right to be identified as author of the work and to object to any derogatory treatment of it.

Licensing entitlement: so that you as copyright owner can grant licences for dealings with the work – and on agreed financial terms.

Contract law: which can aid you in informal and formal dealings with publishers attempting to 'call the shots'.

Law of confidence: which can protect the material you discuss with a third party.

Debt-collecting procedures: to help you to obtain due payment with minimum fuss and expense.

Wills and trusts: which can safeguard your wishes as regards what happens to your work in the future.

IS THE LAW AN ASS?

For you as the writer, the law can offer constant protection. For example, it usually recognises the existence of your copyright – without which your work could be stolen, copied and/or misused – as the words flow from your pen or printer. The law is also there to construe a contract in any commercial dealings with your work – whether or not this is embodied in a signed document. If you are not paid under such a contract, then redress does exist for you. Therefore, ass or not, the law is of use to you.

However, there is some rough with the smooth. Certain legal sanctions can be very dangerous to writers. The law of libel can trap even the innocent, if careless. A writer may also unknowingly transgress the boundaries of plagiarism. The financial penalty and damage to literary reputation can be disastrous. You need to know when to exercise caution.

WATCHING OUT FOR LEGAL DANGERS

A writer is more at risk from proceedings in that the evidence is always there – written down for all to see. For example, an action for slander (basically, spoken abuse, as opposed to libel which is the written form) may often fail for lack of proof. A writer, however, cannot deny what he said in print.

Main legal danger zones for a writer

- Infringing someone else's copyright, through direct or indirect copying. Although general ideas themselves have no copyright, if you write something too similar to another's work, whether unintentionally or however cleverly paraphrased, there can be problems.

- Quoting too much from another's material or drawing upon specialised research without permission or acknowledgement.

- Libelling someone whether by express reference, by implication or disguised as a fictional character.

- Entering a contract without appreciating onerous terms within it – or even that it is a contract.

- Failing to make adequate provision in your will for what happens to your work, so that your literary affairs become mismanaged and the future of your work suffers.

GAINING THE REWARDS OF KNOWING YOUR RIGHTS

The law is present in your writing career. You can use it, break it or ignore it. The last two are at your peril. The first can mean:

- The fruits of your labours remain your own – not a springboard for others to manipulate.

- You enter contracts with your eyes open, ready to object and negotiate upon any unreasonable terms.

- You do not enter contracts by accident through informal correspondence.

- You receive increased income from safeguarded royalties and licensing arrangements.

- You can take action to secure prompt payment, including proceedings if necessary.

• You can meet force with force in any dispute and, from as strong a position as possible, reach a good settlement.

CASE STUDIES – INTRODUCTION

The fictional case studies below introduce three typical writers whose imaginary situations we will follow in the succeeding chapters. Each works within a different literary field. The law will be the same for each, but because of their particular aims, the implications may affect them in different ways.

Whilst neither the case studies nor any other information in this book can cover specific circumstances which may arise in any individual case (and neither are intended as a substitute for professional advice), they may give you useful pointers relevant to common situations.

Liz Burnett, novelist, short story and article writer

Liz is a fiction writer in her mid-thirties. She has managed to combine domestic commitments with a promising writing career. She began with stories for popular magazines (for which market she still writes occasionally) but now concentrates on novels. She also writes the odd article, usually commissioned through her magazine contacts.

Bill Sellars, poet and biographer

Bill is a former history teacher, in his early sixties. His retirement has given him the opportunity to develop his talent for poetry. He is also producing a biography from research into a local Victorian dignitary.

Daniel Charles, playwright and screen-writer

Daniel is a dramatist in his mid-forties. Although he 'dabbled in writing' from an early age, most of his working life was spent in the army, which he left several years ago because of ill-health. He was always unsettled in his 'civvy-street' job. When made redundant, he decided to concentrate on writing. He attended a residential course with a well-respected organisation and found his forte in drama. His plays have been produced by amateur groups and some material used in radio shows. He is currently working on a sit-com, having received a positive response to his proposal from an independent TV production company.

SUMMARY

Essential law for writers:

- Copyright
- Libel
- Contract
- Litigation
- Wills/trusts

DISCUSSION POINTS

1. Consider whether you have to apply for copyright in your work.

2. Defamation is the collective legal term for libel and slander. Which of these will affect you most as a writer?

3. What kind of dealings with a publisher could potentially amount to a binding contract?

2
Using Your Copyright

... to protect, in as effective and uniform a manner as possible, the rights of authors in their literary and artistic works
(Underlying desire stated in the Berne Convention, as revised)

WHAT IS COPYRIGHT?

Basically it is the right to allow (or not to allow) anyone to copy your work. Under our law, it can arise **automatically** through the mere act of writing. Every original literary work you create is vested magically as it appears in a tangible form with the legal by-product of copyright.

For instance, the above paragraph is now copyright. Similarly neither this book nor any substantial part of it can be reproduced without permission. (There are limited exceptions – see Chapter 3.)

'How can I apply for copyright for my book?' is a common question from novice writers. The answer is 'You don't' (as hopefully you replied to the first Discussion Point in Chapter 1). The confusion often arises because you must apply for a patent for inventions and to register a trade mark. The same formalities do not generally attach to owning copyright in this country.

- Where you produce work **in the course of employment**, copyright usually belongs to your employer, unless there is a contract stating otherwise.

Copyright is in what you write – not what you think

It is very difficult to gain legal protection over mere ideas.

Example

Suppose you discuss the ingenious plot of your next thriller at a writers' seminar. Sometime later you find that the quiet one in the corner has announced that a publisher has accepted his novel based on the same story. This type of situation can rarely give rise to a legal claim.

Always get it down in writing. Then you will gain copyright as regards your own written format and anything very similar can be challenged.

What sort of right is copyright?

As it affects writers, it is mainly 'civil'. This does not mean a civil right like freedom of speech. Here it signifies that you can enforce your rights as an individual through the civil court system (see Chapter 7).

Most rights relevant to writers are civil, as you will see as you progress through this book. In some instances the criminal law steps in, including criminal offences relating to copyright. The police usually only become involved where there is modern-day 'piracy' – for example, unauthorised editions or pirated copies of taped books. Sometimes Trading Standard Departments (you should find the address of your local one in *Yellow Pages*) will implement such prosecutions in the magistrates courts. Private prosecutions *can* be taken out, though some people have taken this step and found it can back-fire, proving embarrassing and costly.

What are the legal remedies?

The orders which the civil courts can make include:

- An injunction – to stop publication of infringing work.

- Damages – to compensate you. (Additional damages can be awarded for flagrant infringement.)

- An account of profits – so that you take over the profits made by an infringing act. (This is an alternative to damages).

- An order for seizure/destruction of items containing the infringement.

You may find that any challenge you make is settled before proceedings have to be commenced (see also Chapter 7). Involving a solicitor will probably add authority to your challenge and 'encourage' a favourable settlement.

How long does copyright last?

Under UK law, the period has for a long time been basically for the author's life plus a further fifty years. A recent European Directive extended the fifty to seventy years, calculated from the end of the calendar year of the author's death. This is intended to harmonise the position throughout Europe. It has recently been implemented here by Parliament through The Duration of Copyright and Rights in Performances Regulations 1995. This has given rise to various complications, particularly regarding 'revived' and 'extended' copyright in some works.

What is copyright worth?

That depends on the saleability of your manuscript. Nevertheless, there may be potential value, even in what you consider to be your minor pieces. If you manage to publish several novels, you may find the short stories which you used for 'teething' are attractive to a publisher for an anthology.

● **Resist** any attempt by a publisher to obtain full copyright and control over your works (see Chapter 5).

How do you prove copyright?

If the work is published in the UK, there is little problem in establishing legal protection. But how do you prove that you wrote an unpublished work before anyone else?

Some organisations offer a service of registering unpublished works on a database for a fee. This might be seen as an excessive precaution to have to take. If you could only prove your right through such measures it would go against the spirit of the Berne Convention (discussed later). This stresses that no formal procedure should be necessary to gain copyright.

In any dispute, however, the courts might find it difficult to grant you an order, if simply faced with 'one word against another'. In civil cases, the onus of proof is upon the individual making a claim to prove his allegations on a balance of probabilities. You must bring some evidence to sway the balance. Items such as diary notes have been used in court. Witnesses may be available; for example, someone to whom you showed your manuscript for critical comment. Don't forget that your own testimony is still some evidence, though obviously the self-interest factor makes it carry less weight.

For important work over which you are very concerned, a precaution can be to post a sealed copy to yourself and retain this unopened with its dated postmark. (It is also there as a back-up hard copy in real emergencies. Jilly Cooper tells how she left the only copy of a manuscript on a bus and had to rewrite the lot – though it still became a bestseller.)

What about copyright notices?

The familiar © symbol is prescribed by the Universal Copyright Convention (see later) and is a necessary part of claiming copyright in some countries. Whilst not a legal necessity here, it is still useful to include on your material as a 'warning shot' that you will actively guard your copyright. It can also help you defeat a defence of **innocent infringement** (such as when someone maintains that they genuinely did not know that copyright subsisted in the work) and thus allow you to recover damages.

You can simply insert

© 1996 by (*your name*)

or go further by also adding a clause similar to Figure 1. (As regards the 1988 legislation mentioned, you will study this later in this chapter.)

All rights reserved. No part of this work may be reproduced in any material form (including photocopying or storing it in any medium by electronic means) without the written permission of the copyright owner except in accordance with the provisions of the Copyright, Designs and Patents Act 1988. Any unauthorised act in this respect may lead to legal proceedings, including a civil claim for damages.

Fig. 1. Copyright notice.

What are the origins of copyright?

Parliament has recognised this right since the eighteenth century. Until recently it has been treated in this country as primarily a type of property right. It is perhaps significant of our mercantile past that UK law has, in one sense, seen creativity as a commodity. Copyright is referred to technically as a type of **intellectual property**. The rest of Europe has probably had a more altruistic recognition of the creator's right, through, for example, *droite de suite* (resale royalty rights) and *droits moraux* (moral rights) which have existed there for some time.

RIGHTS	SECTION
Copyright – the 'property right' which exists in every original literary, dramatic, musical or artistic work.	1
The exclusive right to copy the work and issue copies of it to the public.	2, 17 and 18
The exclusive right to perform, show or play the work in public.	2 and 19
The exclusive right to broadcast the work or include it in a cable programme service.	2 and 20
The exclusive right to make an adaptation of the work.	2 and 21
The right (a) to assign (i.e. sell/give) the whole copyright or just some rights (as mentioned above) attached to it, provided it is done in writing and signed by you (b) to give a licence to allow the work to be published or dealt with in a particular way (c) to leave your copyright to a specified person in your will.	90
The right to assign/license copyright in future works.	91
Moral rights.	77 – 89

Fig. 2. Table of rights in the Copyright, Designs and Patents Act 1988.

The international background has come to influence our law, particularly through **conventions** (types of charter) signed by several countries. The four main copyright conventions are:

- Berne
- Universal Copyright
- Rome
- Geneva.

Only the first two really affect literary copyright. Of those, Berne gives greater protection to authors.

The idea behind these conventions is that the countries involved will regulate the rights of authors in similar ways. There is also impetus for harmonisation from the European Community.

The Act

These influences were partly behind the introduction of the **Copyright, Designs and Patents Act 1988**. If you remember only one technical legal authority, make it this one. It is 'the Act' and is referred to as such in the rest of this chapter. Your rights under it are the cards in your hand when you negotiate any deal with a publisher.

Figure 2 lists the main rights together with the section of the Act in which each appears.

KNOWING YOUR 'MORAL RIGHTS'

What are your moral rights?

Every law student learns – if they did not know already – that law and morality are never the same. The one can, however, influence the other. For example, Victorian morality upheld the law which sent Oscar Wilde to prison for homosexuality and which later more liberal attitudes helped abolish. As regards copyright, 'moral rights' is a technical term for **legal provisions aimed at preserving an author's literary reputation**.

At one time, the only moral rights which the English courts recognised in this area seem to have been their own. They would not enforce copyright protection for a work which they regarded as immoral. Just after the First World War, a novel was viewed by a judge as portraying adultery too attractively. The author was denied legal redress for breach of copyright. Such attitudes took effect more as arbitrary censorship (later blasted away by the 1960s trial concerning the novel *Lady Chatterley's Lover*). They did not give much recognition to the status of the writer.

The Act brought express moral rights. These are:

- **The right to be identified as the author** when the work is published, performed, broadcast, included in a film or sound recording, or adapted.

- **The right to object to derogatory treatment of work** through something being inserted or deleted, or any other alteration or adaptation made when it is published, performed, broadcast or included in a cable programme, film or sound recording.

- **The right not to be falsely attributed as author of work**.

Why are these important?

Paternity right

This is the name for the first moral right listed above (perhaps sexist, but accepted terminology). It is essential to get credit for your work at every opportunity. An example is, of course, when sales in a novel increase following dramatisation on television. The author needs to be properly credited, especially if the adaptation has a different title from the original. (For example, Stephen King's short story, *The Body*, which was not in his most characteristic style, formed the basis for the successful film, *Stand By Me*.)

Integrity right

This is the second moral right. Whilst it may not have the same economic worth as the paternity right, it matters a great deal to writers. There are easier ways of making money, and the writer is usually also motivated by the need to communicate a particular idea in a particular way. To see that distorted can be devastating. It is said that Anthony Burgess was mortified at the film adaptation of *A Clockwork Orange*. (This was pre-Act.) There have also been Hollywood battles involving committed directors, such as Terry Gillam, who wished his – rather than Universal Studios' – version of *Brazil* to be released. Artistic and commercial interests often clash. Changes detrimental to a work can injure the creator's credibility and career.

Objections

You cannot object to every change made to your work (otherwise editors would be out of a job). Treatment is only 'derogatory' if it

distorts or mutilates your work or prejudices your 'honour or reputation'. The case law is limited, but what seems to be involved is something which changes the artistic impact. For example, a director cut a specific stage direction for a West End production of Samuel Beckett's *Footfalls*. The direction indicated that a character should walk several paces forward and back during the play. The estate of the playwright (acting through his agent) objected and successfully insisted that this be put back in. Given the title and the author's reputation, there must be a strong argument that a stage direction of this sort was vital to the integrity of the work.

Exception
• There is no paternity or integrity right over work for publication in a newspaper, magazine, periodical, encyclopaedia, or other collective work or for news broadcasts. This is therefore relevant to many freelance writers.

False attribution
The third moral right protects you against false attribution. It will mainly apply when you are rich and famous, and someone falsely insinuates that you are the author of work, in order to trade on your reputation.

PRESERVING THESE RIGHTS

You must **assert in writing your right to be identified as author**. This could be by a small print notice on your work such as:

> The right of (*insert your name*) to be identified as author of this work, pursuant to s 77 of the Copyright, Designs and Patents Act 1988, is hereby asserted.

You can assert the right in relation to a pen name – but you must specify this.

It is important not to accidentally forgo moral rights, such as through implication in correspondence. This might, for example, arise if a publisher wrote to you offering a fee for 'full rights' and you accepted without clarifying this phrase. This is because, in law, something known as an 'estoppel' can arise to prevent you going back on something agreed, whatever your true intention at the time. Another example might be if a publisher sent you a form including a waiver (letting-go) of your rights, which you returned unsigned but without expressly rejecting it, and meanwhile agreed to publication over the telephone.

AVOIDING INFRINGEMENT OF COPYRIGHT

Whilst the law protects your work, there is a corresponding obligation upon you not to infringe the rights of others. If you wish to use or draw upon another's work, pay heed to the following guidelines:

- First consider whether the work is still copyright or in 'the public domain' (i.e. copyright has expired). This is obvious with, for example, Shakespeare, but be especially careful with more recent writers from the late nineteenth century onwards. The new seventy-year period has brought complicated transitional provisions, including 'revived' and 'extended' copyrights.

- Note also, that a publisher can sometimes claim copyright in a typographical arrangement. This copyright lasts for **twenty-five years**.

- If the work is in copyright, then copying it is restricted (see Chapter 3).

- If you infringe copyright by accident, when you did not know and had no reason to believe there was copyright in the work, you may have the defence of innocent infringement. Usually you are not ordered to pay compensation (though publication of your infringing work will normally be stopped).

CASE STUDIES

Liz is 'robbed'

Liz naturally had several short story rejections in addition to her acceptances. She is shocked to find that a 'twist' story which she failed to place has appeared in a magazine under someone else's name.

Liz's records show that this story was rejected two years ago by a magazine based in the same building and being part of the same company group, as the one publishing the story. She suspects the editor who returned it as unsuitable, of giving a copy to a colleague. Then she notices something familiar about the name under which the story appears. She recalls it was a pen name used by a member of a writers' group she formerly attended. She and the member had swapped work for mutual criticism, until this person shunned her after Liz began to have some success.

The editor proves to be a red herring. (Whilst many editors work under tight budgets and are not necessarily saint-like individuals, most are professionals who would not risk reputation through such shoddy behaviour.) The real villain is the jealous ex-friend, who is finding it difficult to get anywhere by her own efforts. Liz has the evidential burden of showing that she wrote the story. A rejection may prove of use for once. The editor is unlikely to remember or wish to become involved, but the rejecting letter may provide corroboration. Liz may possibly have the statement of another third party to whom she showed the story, together with her original drafts and computer data.

Her most effective course is to approach the magazine publishing the story. It will probably be anxious to avoid litigation/bad press and promote a settlement. Liz should hold out for a reasonable amount as regards the lost fee and opportunity for publication under her name. It may be possible to negotiate that the magazine print one of her other stories at a future date.

Bill wants to 'borrow'

In the biography of his eminent Victorian, Bill wants to quote several long passages from the diary of a nineteenth-century contemporary.

Bill needs to establish whether the diary is still in copyright. As a starting point, he will have to check the year of death of the diarist and add on seventy years from the end of that year.

Bill may have a problem because the copyright could still be in existence and possibly have been 'extended' or 'revived' by the recent legal changes. The provisions are very complicated, so he must be careful. Other relevant factors here may be whether the diary was published or not, and whether published posthumously, as this can, in some circumstances, affect the duration of copyright. To be on the safe side, Bill may have to approach the diarist's descendants or publisher (if any) to ascertain who is the present copyright owner, and obtain permission. If he decides instead simply to mention the fact of the association of his subject with the diarist, then he need not take these steps.

Daniel is adaptable

One of Daniel's plays is staged by a small company and receives favourable local press coverage. A radio station approaches him to adapt and broadcast this. At first he is flattered and gives his consent. This particular play, however, is a little more than his usual comedy pieces. It includes some political satire which the station intends to cut. He is therefore having second thoughts.

Daniel should argue over this on the basis of his integrity right. Treatment is, however, only derogatory if it amounts to a distortion or mutilation of the play or damages Daniel's 'honour or reputation'. He could try to contest that to remove the serious element will damage his reputation if the work now appears merely flippant.

The best solution is probably for Daniel to discuss the matter with the station. As he wants the broadcast to go ahead, Daniel should avoid being adversarial. He should aim for a compromise, whereby some of the producer's reservations are taken into account but with as few cuts to the text as possible.

SUMMARY

- Under our law, you usually obtain copyright automatically in what you write. Always get it down on paper/disc/beermat – whatever you choose – as soon as you can.

- Whilst not a UK legal requirement, putting a copyright notice on your work, such as the familiar © followed by name and year can 'warn-off' would-be copiers and help defeat their defence of innocent infringement.

- If very concerned that your unpublished work could be copied, post a sealed copy to yourself so that it bears the date of posting (or leave it with, for example, a bank or solicitor, obtaining their dated receipt) to provide evidence of when it was written by you.

- The Copyright, Designs and Patents Act 1988 gives you rights which are your bargaining tools in negotiating any contract.

- Your paternity right has to be asserted in writing. Include this in any contract with a publisher (see also Chapter 5).

- Beware of formal arrangements which imply that you forgo any of your 'moral rights'.

- If you wish to draw upon another writer's material, check

whether it is in copyright. If so, follow the guidelines given in Chapter 3.

DISCUSSION POINTS

1. If you were in a similar position to Liz in the case study, what sort of evidence could you bring to support your case? Consider how you deal with your work, with a view to keeping simple records of its development, copies and details of submissions with dates.

2. Devise a simple copyright notice in small font, consisting of at least ©, your name and the year, to position discreetly on your work.

3. What sort of unauthorised changes to your work (beyond normal editing) would you regard as infringing your integrity right?

3
Utilising Material

...laws were like cobwebs; where the small flies were caught, and the great break through.

(Apothegms, Francis Bacon)

INPUTTING SOURCES WITHIN YOUR TEXT

By and large, facts, news, general ideas and information do not have copyright. On the face of it, therefore, you have a free hand when it comes to the sources you wish to build upon in your work.

That said, you must be careful if you are basing your work, or part of it, on lines similar to those of another which is in copyright. If you are a non-fiction writer, for example, you must go back to the original authorities rather than rely on any existing book which you are trying to better/rival. Mere paraphrasing, however careful, is always dangerous and unethical.

Selection
This also applies as regards the selection of material. For example, if you wanted to write a book of questions and answers on technical matters, you cannot take the framework used in a similar work. You must structure your own questions and answers from scratch.

Presentation
The presentation of factual information can be protected by copyright. One judge said this depended upon 'the requisite degree of skill, judgement and labour' which had gone into selection and presentation. Particular care must be taken as regards lists or tables, or when you take information from any catalogue. You must use your own individual layout.

Acknowledgement
It is safest and professional courtesy to acknowledge sources.

This is not really required where information is **common knowledge**. Sometimes it is difficult to be sure if this is the case, or whether only the skill and labour of another author made the data available. If in doubt, acknowledge (see later).

HOW MUCH CAN YOU QUOTE?

A matter of some substance

You can be guilty of an infringement if you use without permission any **substantial part** of a work in copyright.

The courts look at the circumstances in each case. Even a tiny part can be enough if it is the crux of the original work. A film company infringed copyright by using twenty seconds of a four-minute tune without permission. In another case, however, the use of four lines of a song as chapter headings was allowed. It is neither quality nor quantity that matters, but what the courts see as **substantiality**.

A few short words

Fortunately writers are helped by the **de minimus rule**. (This is the first lawyer's Latin encountered in this book. You will get used to it.) It means that the courts will not interfere with the use of small and trivial pieces of another's work.

Basically this has the effect that names, short phrases and brief titles will not usually be given protection. For example, in one case the judge felt that the authoress of *The Wombles* could not claim a monopoly in that name. In another case it was not possible to claim copyright over a single invented word.

Titles are often duplicated. The phrase 'The Eye of the Storm', for example, has been used by both Nobel prize-winning novelist, Patrick White, and thriller writer, Jack Higgins. As long as such words basically do not **pass-off** (disguise) one work as that of a different author, or mislead the public, there is usually no problem. Descriptive titles such as *Business Accounting* are safe. Be more wary of distinctive ones like *The Importance of Being Earnest*.

Similar passing-off considerations apply as regards any name under which you publish.

A famous pop group recently tried to stop publication of an unauthorised book about them by claiming use of their name was a breach of trademark. The High Court did not agree. It remains to be seen if there may be any further legal developments in this area.

Longer extracts

Using longer extracts from another work in copyright can be dangerous without permission. In one case the taking of 600 words from a 200-page book was held to be an infringement. Even smaller amounts are unlikely to be tolerated by the courts if used in a rival work. They usually look askance at any work which competes and takes revenue away from something from which it 'borrows'. There is some flexibility if the use ranks as fair dealing.

Fair dealing

Firstly, fair dealing can cover **research and private study**. For example, you may resort to a reference library whilst working on an historical novel, and need to take notes from textbooks. This is technically a 'permitted act'.

Writers are more concerned, however, with fair dealing which covers **criticism, review and news reporting**. It is thought possibly to extend to more general areas such as illustrating a point and putting forward an argument. Acknowledgement is required.

If fair dealing, you are allowed to take more of someone else's work. Just how much, only the courts can say for sure in each situation. Nevertheless, useful guidance was given through an agreement between the Society of Authors and the Publishers Association. The basis of this is:

- When taking a single prose extract, do not exceed 400 words.

- With a series of prose extracts, do not exceed 300 words for each and take no more than 800 words in all.

- In quoting poetry, do not use more than 40 lines and no more than a quarter of the whole poem in any event.

Fair dealing does not apply to extracts used for an anthology. Then you must obtain express permission for **any** quotation of copyright material.

Quoting accurately

If quoting from another's work, do so precisely. The courts have regarded it as extremely serious to miss out a single 'not' or to replace 'or' with 'and'.

ACKNOWLEDGING YOUR SOURCES

If you include a quotation either with permission or as fair dealing, you must give a sufficient acknowledgement which preferably should at least **identify the author and title** of the work from which it is taken. This can be in your main text – perhaps in brackets – or as a footnote.

As regards sources generally, a traditional approach is to mention the author of the source by his last name, within your main text, and then to give full details of his work in a bibliography.

You can also insert a sweeping-up clause where you are not sure if you have used matters of **common knowledge** or not. This is useful for compilations, books of records/facts, or newspapers. An example is given in Figure 3.

Except where specifically acknowledged, the information included in this work is believed to be 'common knowledge' and its source is many and varied. Whilst there has been no verbatim use of copy, it is possible that some has been gleaned from publications such as (*insert names of publications, authors and publishers*) and this is gratefully acknowledged.

Figure 3. Sample clause relating to general sources

AVOIDING PLAGIARISM

What is plagiarism?
Plagiarism is not a technical legal term. It derives from the Latin for 'kidnapping'. It commonly means the appropriating of another's ideas or work. It is often used by writers and publishers loosely to cover not only straightforward copying but also the 'stealing' of basic ideas and plots. (There is, however, an academic argument against breach of copyright being within the legal definition of theft.)

How can you prevent being plagiarised?
As you have seen, copyright is in the written form, rather than general ideas. It is also widely felt that there is a finite number of plots (boy meets girls, rags to riches and so on) with permutations. Therefore it is difficult to obtain legal protection from this form of plagiarism, without very close similarity.

Other sanctions can exist, such as bad press and damage to literary reputation. The standing of the great short story writer, Katherine Mansfield, was affected for a time by such suggestions regarding similarity between one of her stories and one by Chekhov. (She may even have suffered blackmail over this.)

Hitting on the same idea as someone else frequently happens. There seem to be trends in creativity.

In protecting your own original ideas/information from less coincidental circumstances, the law of confidence can help in certain situations.

The law of confidence

This is often used by inventors or designers to protect confidential information to safeguard commercial 'know-how'. It can sometimes help in situations where discussions need to be confidential, such as between author and publisher, or taking a programme idea to a television producer.

One example arises from a case concerning certain actresses who described an idea for a programme about a female rock band (later made as *Rock Follies*) to a script writer, who passed it to a producer and TV company. They were successful in court when the programme was later developed without them.

Although lawyers agree that this law exists, there is an academic squabble over what type it is. It may be:

- a right implied into a contract,

- a tort (civil wrong) preventing disclosure of anything confidential,

- a property right, *or*

- based upon equitable principles of good faith.

The last is the most probable. Under this, someone in possession of confidential information is regarded as like a trustee and has a duty not to let that information pass into the wrong hands nor to exploit it without permission.

To get protection from this law, you are on strong ground if you can show that:

- the type of information involved is usually treated as confidential

- the information was revealed in confidential circumstances

- it was then used without your authority.

This was indicated by a leading case – *Coco* v. *Clark* (1969). The courts do not always completely follow these guidelines. In the famous *Spycatcher* case, an order was granted even though the information (the contents of the book) could hardly be described as confidential any longer.

Using this law

The law may apply where you have a relationship with a publisher or an agent and allow them to be privy to your ideas for a new book. Certain steps can be taken to strengthen any case you might have:

• Make it clear in any contact, correspondence, discussions or negotiations that you regard the subject matter as confidential.

• Write down your idea (oral ideas are more difficult to protect), and consider lodging a copy with a third party like your bank/ solicitor to show you thought of this and when.

• Keep a record of the time you spent developing the idea.

• Keep copies of correspondence and records of meetings, discussions, etc. (Reconstructed diaries have sometimes been used in court as evidence.)

• Get an express clause in any contract to the effect that relevant discussions are confidential (see Chapter 5).

Legal remedies under the law of confidence are similar to those regarding copyright (see Chapter 2).

Could you be a plagiarist?

You will hopefully follow the guidelines given to help you avoid breach of copyright. Also be careful to avoid too much similarity in general to any other work.

There have been instances of whole books being 'borrowed', with a few factors like names and location changed. Underneath, the original was still well-recognisable. No writer worth his/her salt would stoop to such unethical practice – at least knowingly.

There is some recognition of the phenomena of 'subconscious copying'. We all imbibe influences from what we read. The genius of T. S. Eliot's poetry exploited this to full effect. It can be that an author reads a book decades earlier and then reproduces it later believing it to be original. Unfortunately, it is very difficult to take measures to control your subconscious. At least be aware of the main works within your genre and steer clear of close similarity.

PHOTOCOPYING

Photocopying material which is in copyright is technically restricted. You are generally allowed to copy a reasonable portion of a book (usually about one chapter) or 5 per cent of a literary work for your own research and private study. This falls within fair dealing.

The restrictions are important when it comes to voluminous copying. (Otherwise writers, including you, would lose potential royalties.) The Copyright Licensing Agency was set up to help control the situation. It issues licences to such bodies as educational authorities, business concerns, and more recently the Home Office in return for a fee.

As a book author, you should receive an appropriate share of such fees. These can be remunerative for frequently consulted non-fiction. Payment in respect of magazines and journals, however, usually all goes to the publisher.

UNDERSTANDING DATA PROTECTION

If you compile computer data, be aware of **The Data Protection Act 1984**.

This covers **personal data** – basically personal information about someone else, held on computer. It includes mailing lists and could stretch to information collected in research or interviews about named subjects, or relating to individual agents, editors or publishers.

The legislation sets out principles regarding how information is obtained, stored and disclosed. It stresses the need for information to be obtained fairly to prevent methods like telephone deception (now a criminal offence).

The Data Protection Registrar receives applications from those who wish to hold personal data. The following is required for the register:

• name and address

• description of the data

• purpose for which data is held

- sources from which data was obtained

- people to whom data may be disclosed

- countries where data may be transferred

- the address where data subjects (people about whom information is held) can obtain access to the data.

A fee is payable.

Unregistered holding of personal data is an offence. If you are unsure whether you should register, contact the Data Protection Registry (see addresses at the back of this book). You can obtain explanatory leaflets from them and help with specific queries.

Data subjects can request from you a copy of information held about them. You can charge a reasonable administrative fee, but if the information is inaccurate, they can claim compensation. European regulations may extend such matters to manual filing and bring any new requirements for consent to disclosure.

CASE STUDIES

Liz carries out a study

Liz is commissioned by a magazine to write on women's experiences in relation to maternity rights.

She interviews several women, recording their names, addresses, details of employment and the maternity benefits which they received. In her article, Liz states no names but describes their situations and draws overall conclusions. Each woman's permission has been obtained for this.

Liz must be mindful of the Data Protection Act. It is the information stored on her computer which is relevant to this – not her article. She may have to register with the Data Protection Registry and should contact them to check. Registration will probably be applicable, even if she deletes the names and addresses from her PC, but retains some method, such as codes, by which she can identify the subjects. She may fall within an exemption because her data subjects are not identified in the results of her research, but this will depend on the circumstances and the purpose for which she wishes to retain data.

Bill backs it up with statistics

In writing the biography, Bill comes across a recent publication which gives statistics illustrating the average life-span and health of Victorian males.

Bill wishes to use these statistics to illustrate the expectations and quality of life which the subject of his biography would have. He intends to include a table from the text concerned in his own work.

Although Bill is using facts, over which there is usually no copyright, the table is the result of skill and labour by the writer and it will almost certainly be copyright. Using the whole format is unlikely to be within fair dealing. Bill should obtain consent, through approaching the publisher's Permissions Department. He may have to pay a fee. The exact amount depends upon the author/publisher concerned, the likely print run of Bill's book and the countries where it may be sold.

If Bill has not yet found a publisher, he could leave his application until later. His publisher may possibly agree to pay the cost or this section of the biography may be edited out anyway.

Daniel's great idea

Daniel is negotiating with an independent TV company on his proposed sit-com. It centres upon the catering corps and the 'ups and downs' in the life of an eccentric army cook.

As far as Daniel is aware, nothing on these lines has been done before. He has developed the idea, discussed it with the producer (who has indicated that Daniel will be commissioned for the screen play) and written a first draft. The TV company discuss this with him, then suddenly tell him they have decided not to pursue the project. It is not until sometime later that Daniel learns that they are continuing with it but have taken on a new writer.

Daniel may have a claim under the law of confidence, because he discussed his idea in circumstances of confidentiality. The *Rock Follies* case would certainly support his position. He should strongly protest. If necessary, he should threaten proceedings (which could potentially halt the programme/award him substantial damages), and aim to be reinstated as screen writer, if he so wishes, or otherwise obtain a large out-of-court settlement (see Chapters 6 and 7).

SUMMARY

- In drawing upon research always re-work this, going direct to original sources, and devising your own form of presentation.

- To quote from a work which is in copyright, the only foolproof way is to obtain permission from the copyright owner.

- Short phrases, names and titles can, however, normaliy be used without permission.

- If you are 'fair dealing', no permission is required but stay within the word limits mentioned in this chapter and give an acknowledgement.

- Acknowledge your sources preferably with at least the author's name and title.

- Stress confidentiality of proposals with publishers/agents and anyone else with whom you enter discussions.

- Bear in mind the Data Protection provisions as regards your computer data.

DISCUSSION POINTS

1. List the circumstances when it might be said that 'facts can be copyright'.

2. Consider whether you could adopt a pen name of Freddy Forsyth.

3. In your novel, you want to quote twelve lines of a modern poem. Consider which circumstances might make it advisable to seek permission.

4
Avoiding Libel

Beyond the redemption of the courts.
> Diplock LJ's comment on the law of libel
> in *Slim* v. *Daily Telegraph Ltd* (1968)

WHAT IS LIBEL?

Libel is one part of the law of defamation. The other part is slander. Broadly speaking, libel is written, slander is spoken. Both involve statements which are **defamatory** – basically insulting to reputation.

Playing the game
To understand libel properly, you must look at the legal rules involved. 'Rules' is an apt term. They are devious and elaborate. It is no surprise that a board game was marketed under the title 'Libel'. A well-known *Coronation Street* actor was involved in the promotion, himself fresh from successful litigation.

Before judge and jury
Defamation is a tort, i.e. a civil wrong as opposed to a crime. In rare circumstances, it can be a crime if it leads to a breach of the peace, or if it creates an offence such as treason or sedition.

Writers are mainly troubled by the civil version, for which a slandered or libelled person may sue in the High Court. Like a criminal trial, a judge and jury are involved, which is one reason why it is expensive (new law may alter this in some cases). No legal aid is given, however poor or deserving the aggrieved party may be.

The expense is a deterrent as regards those who might wish to sue you over something you have written. If you are sued, however, the financial risk to you is high. In the past, juries have sometimes stipulated massive amounts of damages to send out a message as well as give compensation. Recently, certain libel damages awarded to Elton John were cut. The Court of Appeal gave new guidelines which may prevent very high awards in cases not involving personal integrity. At the time of writing, the anticipated new Defamation Act may also help reduce legal costs by simplifying procedure particularly for claims under £10,000. Nevertheless, the pecuniary penalty for libel is not insubstantial. You may also have to pay the other party's costs too, in addition to being saddled with an injunction preventing future publication of the work involved.

HOW FAR CAN YOU GO?

In what you write
Writers are obviously more at risk from libel rather than from slander. Less obvious is what this includes. Whereas slander is mainly speech in an unrecorded form, libel can be through not only literature, but also work broadcast on radio and television, the performance of a play or illustrations. Therefore **any form your work takes** is capable of containing libel. That probably includes electronic forms. Libel by, for example, e-mail may be more difficult to prove, but a large supermarket chain recently had to reach an out-of-court settlement on such a claim, and there have been similar cases arising in the USA.

In what you do with it
For there to be any claim, material **has to be published**. This includes self-publishing, small press, competition anthologies, writers' circle magazines and merely showing your work to any third party. The reading aloud of written work at a writers' workshop is sufficient.

A book involves a series of 'publications' for legal purposes:

- the author submitting the work to the publisher
- the work being passed to the printer
- the work being passed to the distributor
- the work being passed down the chain to the bookseller
- the work reaching the public.

The middle-men cannot be sued for libel, providing they were careful and knew nothing of it. Those at the top of the chain – you and your publisher – are always at risk.

In what you say
There is no libel unless the work is defamatory. For this, it must harm

someone's reputation **or** cause that person to be shunned or avoided, in the opinion of right-thinking members of the community. This is why a jury is traditionally required at any hearing. It represents 'right-thinking' and gives its opinion on the effect of the work.

Therefore references such as to dishonesty, immorality or insanity will be potentially libellous. So too will suggestions of someone having an infectious disease or being bankrupt, because these things tend to cause a person (rightly or wrongly) to be shunned by others.

In how you say it

Libel need not be express. It can also be by implication (or what the law terms 'innuendo'). A waxwork was once found defamatory because nearby was a 'Chamber of Horrors' sign. Watch not only what you say, but how you say it.

In whom you say it about

It is commonly thought safe to libel the dead. It is true that their right to sue cannot be 'inherited' by anyone else. But think first about whether 'talking ill of the dead' could reflect on the deceased's relatives. For example, a statement that the late Mr A. Aardvark was a bigamist could implicate his last known wife in a similar offence.

It is usually safe to be derogatory of organs of central government and local authorities, as they cannot sue for libel. Implied criticism, however, of particular officers would lead to action. If your motives are malicious, you could also be sued for 'injurious falsehood'.

Generalisations over a large class of people are reasonably risk-free; for example, 'All editors are idiots' – unless there was an implication within the context that your remark was directed at a certain individual. A case where someone objected to a dictionary definition of the word 'jew' failed because he could not show that it referred to him in particular. (This was before modern race relations legislation.)

PREVENTING LEGAL ACTION

The net of libel stretches wide. You must take care to escape from it when first committing your ideas to paper.

Fiction writers may feel that they can hide behind a disclaimer, such as:

> 'All characters in this book are imaginary and any resemblance to any living person is coincidental.'

This carries little legal force. Many publishers do not bother to include it. The court looks at whether the effect of the work was that someone was defamed. Lack of intention to do so or 'coincidental' bad luck is irrelevant to liability (though can help a defence – see later).

Let us consider circumstances which could create a risk.

Pure coincidence

This might be termed 'the nightmare scenario'. You create a brilliant portrayal of a main character. He or she may be villainous, debauched, stupid or barking mad – but definitely imaginary. Yet upon publication, the creation appears in the flesh, like the wrath of Frankenstein, and clutching a libel writ. An old case established there was **liability even where the author did not know of the existence of the person he described**. This concerned a humorous article on a Mr Artemus Jones in Dieppe, accompanied by a lady who was not his wife. In the early twentieth century this was seen as defamatory of a London barrister, who, yes, was called Artemus Jones.

There is a defence available (see later). Your publisher will resent the expense and inconvenience of it and may look to the contract to make you bear any cost involved (see Chapter 5). Basic care should be taken at the outset not to make unintended reference to a living person.

Simple procedural checks can be taken. Suppose, for example, your villain is a fraudulent property surveyor. It is relatively easy to telephone the RICS information desk to check that no one of the same name exists on their register. If your character is identified as coming from or operating within a narrow geographical area, then consult telephone directories in the library. Even if such checks are not foolproof, your carrying them out can help your defence later.

No coincidence

This is where, as a fiction writer, you really are to blame – not so much for intentionally maligning someone, but if you do not bring sufficient creativity into your portrayal to disguise the fact.

Many writers do, of course, start with those people and relationships around them. For some of the greatest, such as Proust and D. H. Lawrence, there seems to have been no other way. Not to do so may be safer, but how much inspiration would be lost as a result? General advice is to write about what you know. Does this have to be confined to flattering your subjects? Fortunately fiction writers aim to create more than a reflection of the actual. In drawing upon life, it is necessary both artistically and legally to adapt and evolve a character.

You should, of course, change names. The use of an unlikely name, however, affords feeble protection if a real person is still recognisable from the text. You should **significantly alter names and background** (even if you feel that no one has been defamed – a jury may disagree).

If the integrity of the work will not suffer, then **consider changing, for example, age and gender**, and including an imagined quirk or two. This is not to say that some similarity to well-known figures cannot be very saleable, as with the Hollywood echoes of Jacqueline Susan's *Valley of the Dolls.* (Strong denials were given, and sales seemed to soar correspondingly.) Fiction must, however, in general, be sufficiently removed from life **so that a sensible reader cannot be expected to connect it with a particular person**.

You could maintain that your readers will not be aware of the actual people upon whom it was based, and therefore no one can claim their reputation has suffered. The law has thought of that one, and **assumes** that 'a sensible reader' will have **knowledge of special facts** which could connect the characters with life.

You could also argue, 'No one agreed with me anyway.' In law it is irrelevant that no reader believed your words to be true. If your writing suggests something defamatory of a person, then that is libel.

DEFENDING LEGAL ACTION

If proceedings are threatened or commenced, there are several effective defences.

'The truth, the whole truth'

It does not normally matter what you say, as long as it is factually true. **Justification** is a complete defence to libel (usually even if the writer acted out of malice). Mistake, however, is not. Stating something **you believe** to be true, even upon good authority, will leave you **liable** if it proves to be **incorrect**.

Ensure the accuracy of sources and keep these available as evidence. The burden of proving that something is true is on you. The court presumes that anything defamatory is untrue until you convince it otherwise. *Private Eye* (no stranger to libel litigation) was caught out when it falsely alleged that the wife of the Yorkshire Ripper had agreed to sell her story to *The Daily Mail* for £25,000. They were ordered to pay a cool £600,000 – but after appeal, the matter was settled at a cold comfort price of £60,000.

'Fair enough'

The other defence which may be available is **fair comment**. This exists to protect freedom of speech. It is particularly relevant to journalists expressing opinion upon **matters of pubic interest**. It also covers critics of books, theatre, film, TV and radio.

In fact, the comment need not be 'fair' in the usual sense. It must simply be what the law regards as 'honest', i.e. **based upon correct facts** and an opinion which an honest man could hold, however prejudiced and obstinate he might be!

The comment must **not be motivated by malice**. The court found a review in *Punch* not fair comment because of ill-will between the reviewer and the author. It may be better for a critic to decline work concerning an artist for whom there is evidence that he holds personal animosity.

'Sorry, honest!'

A special defence is available if you can show your **words were used 'innocently'**. This is basically where you did not know they would defame someone. An 'offer of amends' usually including payment and a **published apology** can sometimes rescue you.

It can also help to support your 'innocence' if you keep early drafts through which a character was developed. Some writers invent a whole biography (as recommended by many tutors). Most of this never features in the main text, but assists the writer to give depth to his protagonist. These notes can show how you created your fiction independently of any real life influences.

Although such evidence is not conclusive and could be fabricated after the event, a court may not automatically doubt your integrity, so such material can provide corroboration if you are challenged.

The anticipated new Defamation Act may bring a new style of 'amends' to simplify the process and possibly make this defence in some ways easier and more favourable, particularly to a publisher.

CASE STUDIES

Liz and the naughty vicar

In an 'aga-saga' style novel, Liz introduces a lecherous clergyman who pursues her married heroine. She has given him the unlikely name of Damien Blennerhassett, and set her story in a fictionalised Cotswold village. A certain Reverend David Blenerhausset from Chipping Camden has now complained.

The similarity in names, coupled with the locality, places Liz on thin ice. The depiction of the character in her novel is potentially libellous. Even if no reader is likely to know the real Reverend Blenerhausset or believe him capable of the conduct of Liz's protagonist, this will not alter the position. It only matters that the words were capable of harming his reputation. However, provided Liz knew nothing of the real vicar (and there appears to be no evidence to suggest that she could have known of him), it may then be possible to placate Reverend Blenerhausset with an appropriate offer of amends.

Bill tells it like it was

In the biography, Bill feels that he must recount certain 'indiscretions' of his otherwise virtuous Victorian. Evidence for this comes from a grandson whom Bill has interviewed in the course of his research. Bill intends to report the stories told by the relative (which have been handed down through the family), and to add his own comments that he is sceptical as to their full validity.

Bill need have no concern as to how this may affect the deceased's reputation (the old adage that you cannot libel the dead). He should, however, consider the nature of the 'indiscretions' and whether stating them could affect anyone else. For example, could they imply that a living person is illegitimate?

The fact that Bill is simply recording statements made by the grandson would not prevent Bill from being sued. Anyone who openly repeats libel in effect publicises it for legal purposes. Bill might have the defence of justification if the reports are true. It is doubtful whether he would be able to prove this as Bill himself seems to doubt them. Furthermore, in commenting on his own scepticism, Bill might imply that the grandson is a liar. Therefore, Bill may be safest to leave out the grandson's information, until he knows that it is more than mere 'hearsay' and he has factual evidence to back it up.

Daniel makes a point

Daniel wishes to dramatise some of his experience in the army, involving a particular officer whom he feels abused his power.

Daniel must proceed very carefully. He would be wise to change the officer's name, age, exact rank and background. For example, he could alter geographical and family origins. He must also make sure that there can be no close identification through association with other characters. Therefore they too must be fictionalised to some extent. In drawing upon his experience, he must also change the exact details of what happened.

SUMMARY

- Make checks that the names which you choose for your characters are not those of similar persons in real-life, for example, in the same profession or geographical area.

- If you draw upon life, change names and background. Consider also altering age and gender and adding different characteristics.

- Ensure your sources of factual information are reliable and keep records of them.

- You can insert a disclaimer like the one set out earlier in this chapter. Bear in mind that, whilst it does no legal harm, it carries little legal strength.

DISCUSSION POINTS

1. Consider whether the following suggestions could be defamatory:

    – that a local council is 'on the take'

    – that a famous actor is to join a cloistered religious sect

    – that a certain businessman is effective but ruthless.

2. You wish to write a wartime novel, which refers to several prominent figures of the time. The plot involves treachery on the part of one of Churchill's aids. When might you have to guard against libel? List the steps you would take to do so.

3. An arch-rival gives a slating and incorrect view of your latest book. In what circumstances can you sue?

5
Entering a Contract

This kindness I will show –
Go with me to a notary, seal me there
Your single bond.

(*Merchant of Venice*, Act 1, Scene 3, Shakespeare)

UNDERSTANDING BASIC CONTRACT LAW

A contract need not always be a signed document. There is, however, a lawyer's saying that 'a verbal contract is not worth the paper it's written on.' The golden rule is **get it in writing**.

What is the vital 'it'? To understand this, you must appreciate the legal basis of any binding agreement – first in relation to **dealings with a magazine**, where the correspondence usually has to do the work. Later you will study contracts with book publishers, where there is more likely to be a formal document to sign.

What is required for a binding contract?
Offer and acceptance
This can be when you offer your manuscript, which the publication accepts. Alternatively, it is arguable that your submission is only 'an invitation to treat'. The publication then offers to publish it at a fee, which you accept. Similarly with commissions, you accept work offered by the editor on specified terms.

Consideration
This is an exchange of promises (or an act in exchange for a promise) worth something to each party. It is your allowing publication in exchange for the promise of payment. Forgoing payment or accepting a nominal sum – as with some small press arrangements – can still be classed as consideration because you gain the benefit of the work being published.

Intention to create legal relations
This is implied in the commercial context of publishing.

Capacity
In general you must be over eighteen, sane and sober when you enter a contract (otherwise special rules apply).

Legality
This is unlikely to affect you. The courts can refuse to enforce any contract which is contrary to legislation or public policy. A contract killing is an extreme example.

Consensus ad idem
This lawyer's Latin means that there must be an agreement without anything, such as misrepresentation, to undermine it. You will cover this area in Chapter 6.

Privity of contract
You have to be a party to a contract to enforce it. Third parties cannot enforce claims under it.

Binding terms

To be enforceable, the terms of any contract must be **certain**. If a magazine uses an imprecise phrase like 'publication subject to space availability', this might be void for uncertainty with no obligation on them to use your work. Aim to **get conditions spelt out**. If the magazine's letter is vague, ensure your reply clarifies the arrangements agreed.

Make clear when payment becomes due. Some magazines pay on acceptance, but on publication is more common. Try to agree payment within seven days of the proposed publication date, time to be of the essence. This will help avoid any 'reasonable time' which could be implied by law, and which is a recipe for debate and late payment.

Confirmation in writing

Editors may not have time to send letters repeating telephone conversations, but there is nothing to stop you sending a note 'just to confirm our discussion' (keeping a copy). It must embody the terms agreed. You cannot unilaterally impose terms. You could devise a standard on your PC, so that despite deadlines, you can find a few minutes to fill in the blanks and get this posted/faxed.

Examples – 'half-commissions'

The need for written confirmation is underlined by the following recent examples. One freelance found that an editor whom she trusted suddenly refused to print or pay for an article he had verbally commissioned. She suspected that he had accidentally double-commissioned it. That should have been his problem, but there was nothing in writing. A major weekly magazine also changed its mind on a star interview, which she had gone to lengths to obtain. Fortunately this commission was confirmed in correspondence. After a few hints at proceedings, she received payment.

Why do you need a contract?

A potentially enforceable contract is a deterrent against unscrupulous editors, who may want features and stories available without giving any commitment to using them.

A legally binding contract is the basis of your getting paid. It is the springboard for taking appropriate action if you do not (see Chapter 7).

- Bear in mind also that the requirements for a contract work both ways. Be careful that your own correspondence does not provide these essential ingredients, if you are merely negotiating and do not yet wish to be bound. If in any doubt, you can head your letters **'subject to contract'** and make it clear that you are not entering into any binding agreement at this stage.

DO YOU NEED AN AGENT?

This is an important question when it comes to book contracts particularly for fiction. It may already be answered. You may have been represented by an agent in placing your manuscript or synopsis. He or she will continue to act on your behalf in negotiating the contract. Nevertheless, you should make the final decisions and approve everything. Therefore you still need to be aware of the main legal implications.

If you do not have an agent, should you get one? You may not have previously approached any, or perhaps you found that they were 'not taking on any new authors at present'. You are unlikely to meet reluctance when a publisher is already keen to sign you up.

The main advantage of having a good agent is the benefit of his/ her experience, negotiating skills and knowledge of publishing practice.

The main disadvantage is the agent's 'cut', which means less financial reward for you.

Making the decision

Although many successful authors are unrepresented, it is probably advisable for new authors to be agented. A good agent can help you structure your writing career from the outset.

The agent must be suitable for your type of writing and for you as an individual. Get references from other writers or any professional bodies you join. (See addresses at the back of this book.)

The agency contract

Most agents will offer you their standard terms. Sometimes this will be in a document for signature, perhaps based on the model form produced by the Association of Author's Agents. If not, make sure you get a letter at least, setting out what has been agreed. Some points to check are:

The agent's commission
This is usually 10 per cent of any British royalties you receive. Around 15 per cent may be reasonable on US rights or other foreign sales.

Termination
Resist any stipulation that suggests that the agency arrangement is 'irrevocable'. An express termination clause, stating how the agency can end, is useful. This could include provision for termination upon either party serving written notice. This will usually be without prejudice to subsisting arrangements. If the agent has, for example, sold a particular book to a publisher then he/she should continue to get the income specified in respect of that book.

Agent's authority
Be clear about the scope you wish to give to the agent. State whether he/she is to handle all your work or just part of it; for example, just novels but not plays.

Stipulate that the agent can negotiate but has no authority to enter a contract for you. (Other types of agent can do this in law.) Be careful not to 'hold-out' (represent) to a publisher that your agent has such power. Otherwise the agent can be seen as having 'ostensible' or apparent authority, and may bind you to something agreed without your consent.

INSISTING ON THE ESSENTIALS

Contracts with publishers

You will probably find that publishers offer you their standard contract.

A few (including some large houses such as Hodder Headline) have adopted a form of the **Minimum Terms Agreement** (MTA) initiated by The Society of Authors and The Writers' Guild. This should be offered to you if you are a member of either.

All contracts depend on individual circumstances. For example, contracts for academic and technical books can be very different. General points are discussed below, but may not apply in every case.

What should you try to ensure is included?

Some of the main points (many already in the MTA) are:

- description of the work including title, length, whether hardback/paperback, illustrations (if any)

- initial print run intended

- an advance (see later)

- royalties (see later)

- anticipated retail price

- provision for made-up accounts every six months and prompt payment of royalties (or a 'pass through clause' for rights income within thirty days, but publishers rarely agree to this)

- provision for you to consent to/be informed of any sub-licences (see later)

- rights to be granted to the publisher or reserved by you (see later)

- a realistic date for the typescript, if the book is commissioned

- the period for the publisher to state changes to the typescript

- a deadline for publication

- a stipulation against change to the title without your consent

- provision for you to be consulted on cover design and other aspects of production

- provision for you to see proofs and make corrections

- provision for you to inspect the publisher's accounts relating to your work

- a review date for the contract; for example, every ten years

- provision for six to twelve free copies and a discount on purchasing more

- an assertion of your paternity right (see Chapter 2)

- provision for a further assertion, copyright notice and prominent credit to you on the title page and cover (with similar provision to be in any sub-licence)

- a termination clause (see Chapter 6)

- a confidentiality clause (see Chapter 3)

Advances
Aim for any advance to be paid on signature (often it will be on publication). It is likely to be based on a proportion of expected earnings from the first print run. Advances vary. You may not even get one.

Royalties
Following the demise of the Net Book Agreement, royalties are likely to be on the basis of the book's recommended retail price. Often they range from 10 per cent to 15 per cent depending on the number of copies involved, with smaller rates paid on children's books and provisions for discounted sales. The publisher may require a net receipt basis. You should then demand a higher rate of 15 per cent or over.

Rights in your work
Some important factors, together with subsidiary rights and their usual publishing terminology, are discussed below, with points on how you might negotiate on these.

Main copyright in your work
Many authors used to assign this outright, with the publisher buying full rights for the copyright period. Some publishers still require this, especially with new writers. (A type of writers' coalition has recently been set up to combat this tendency.) **Resist** if you can, particularly if the chances are that your book may remain in print a long time. Give a **licence** allowing the publisher use of your work for a specified

period. This will usually be exclusive, so that you cannot license it elsewhere at the same time. The publisher is making an investment so will require a reasonable length, perhaps twenty years. Specify the countries where the publisher can use your work.

Sub-licensing
A publisher often grants rights to someone else out of those granted by you. This is important to a publisher's profitability.

Ideally you will want sub-licences to be subject to your consent. The phrase 'such consent not to be unreasonably withheld' often appears in any legal document where consent is mentioned. It effectively means that if you refuse, the publisher could try to obtain a declaration that this is unreasonable and get the court's 'go-ahead' instead.

A more modest goal may be to obtain an agreement that you be consulted before completion of any sub-licence.

Specify your income share. Aim for a minimum 60:40 split in your favour as regards royalties from sub-licensed paperback editions.

US rights and translation rights
These are often retained by authors/their agents to sell elsewhere. If not, the contract should state the income you will receive from these.

Television, radio, film and dramatic rights
These are also often retained by authors/their agents in hope of arranging a profitable deal elsewhere. If granted to a publisher, make sure you receive a high percentage of the proceeds.

Reprographic rights
These relate to photocopying (see Chapter 4). They are usually granted to the publisher, with provision for you to receive a share.

Public Lending Right
Retain this. It was a hard-fought right, which enables authors to receive payment from library borrowing. Income depends on how often your books are taken out, but is not very substantial. To register, obtain a form from the Public Lending Right Office. (See addresses at the back of this book.)

Electronic and mechanical rights
'These are a vital asset which you should safeguard. They may be lucrative in the long run,' says Kay Henning, director of the consultancy, Catalyst Media.

Multimedia is developing rapidly with the new technology, and with it, a whole new language. If you are not already familiar with it, you soon will be. Some key terms, loosely defined, are:

- Internet – a global collection of computers and a possible predecessor to a 'Superhighway'.

- World-Wide Web – name for all documents on the Internet.

- CD-Rom – a compact disc with fixed data.

- CDI – a compact disk with data with which users can interact.

- Infomercials – cross between information and a commercial which you select.

- Interzines – a magazine on the Internet.

- Multimedia – forms of media including the latest technologies.

These could represent a massive market – and your future one – just about to take off.

Therefore electronic publishing rights (in addition to audio and video) are becoming potentially valuable, especially for non-fiction writers. You may be well advised to **retain these**. Having your existing works translated into the new forms could be a beneficial opportunity. Many publishers are already exploiting their 'back catalogues' of older books to relaunch them in a CD-Rom form.

If you do assign these rights, ensure your contract includes good royalties on them.

You could also try to secure an option to produce any CD-Rom background data, later required for your work.

Electrocopying
Some pundits see electronic books as the death knell of copyright, because the new technologies allow users (or 'browsers') to take material so easily.

Don't despair. There are signs that the problems are starting to be addressed. The CLA (see Chapter 3) has, for example, introduced an Electronic Protocol for its schools' licence. Hologram technology may soon be used to protect CDs from being copied. New technology may help with the Internet. Trading Standards have always tried to crack down on piracy. The European Commission is considering measures to regularise the legal position for multimedia. The law may have been left behind but is catching up.

First serial rights
These relate primarily to periodical publications. They are the rights which you should normally give when selling stories or articles to magazines and newspapers, rather than assigning full copyright.

First serial rights apply if the work has not been previously published. Depending on the country involved, they may be referred to as First British Serial Rights, First US Serial Rights, First Australian Serial Rights and so on.

Second serial rights
These are similar but relate to work previously published (even if not just once but several times). They may be included in a book contract to cover, for example, where a publisher of non-fiction uses extracts in a journal. If so, you ought to specify a good royalty rate on these.

Miscellaneous rights
Other rights may be included (or reserved) in the contract. Examples are:

- condensation rights for magazines
- strip cartoon rights
- TV, radio and recorded readings
- one-shot periodical
- condensation rights for books
- merchandising
- promotional reprint rights
- hardcover reprint
- loose leaf and large print
- anthology and quotation rights

The contract should specify the percentage you will receive on each, ideally not less than 50 per cent, with more on some – particularly merchandising.

Catch-all
A 'safety-net' clause should be included stating that all rights not specifically granted to the publisher are reserved by you.

AMENDING THE SMALL PRINT

How successful you may be at negotiating amendments to a publisher's standard contract depends upon your own/your agent's bargaining power and ability. You may find that it contains nothing too disadvantageous – but do **read it**. The case of *Interfoto* v. *Stilletto* (1988) indicated that any very unusual or onerous clause should be specifically drawn to the attention – but you should always first check through anything you sign.

Figure 4 lists some sample clauses which you are likely to encounter, divided into those which are probably acceptable and those which you may wish to resist. (The circumstances of each individual's case may, however, make the boundaries less distinct.)

Getting advice
The guidelines given here are to give you general pointers. Seek advice on the specifics from sources such as an agent and/or a solicitor. The most suitable lawyer will be an IP (Intellectual Property) specialist – unfortunately likely to be the most costly. The Society of Authors or the Writers' Guild may also be able to advise and vet the contract.

Negotiating
Haggling for amendments is an art. You must be sensitive to the position and diplomatic enough not to alienate your publisher through petty objections or delay. Most publishers should not be affronted by reasonable requests which are phrased in a polite and professional manner.

CASE STUDIES

Liz loses an editor
For several years, Liz has sold stories to a particular magazine fiction editor. She recently received an acceptance for her latest stating 'our usual terms apply'. She later received a letter saying that the editor had left, editorial policy had changed and Liz's fiction was no longer suitable.

Liz can do nothing to compel the magazine to take future stories but should press for the latest to be published/paid for. She must show a contract for this based on the acceptance letter. 'Our usual terms apply' could be too uncertain. If, however, Liz has earlier correspondence clearly showing 'a previous course of dealings' she may be able to claim that specific terms are implied. These might relate to a standard fee and payment arrangement.

A change of editor does not usually negate any contract. The editor here was acting as a representative of the magazine company,

REASONABLE	UNREASONABLE
Warranty by you that the work is original, unpublished, does not infringe copyright, is not libellous and, for non-fiction, is accurate, (plus an indemnity if it proves otherwise).	An 'acceptance clause' making publication subject to acceptance of the typescript. This can mean the contract just shows intent to consider publication. (Difficult clause to negotiate upon.)
Right of first refusal over your next book. This may be preferable to your giving an option to the publisher.	A contribution from you towards production costs. (This may indicate you are dealing with so-called 'vanity-press'.)
The publisher is to have control over production.	You are not even to be consulted on production.
With non-fiction particularly, your promise not to produce competing work while this is in print.	A prohibition against you producing any similar work, so precluding, for example, short articles.
Publisher's right to 'remainder' (dispose of surplus copies very cheaply, usually to a remainder merchant).	No minimum time before remaindering, no royalties on remainders nor option for you to purchase surplus instead.

Fig. 4. Table of sample contract clauses.

not in a personal capacity.

Bill is 'signed-up'

After many rejections, Bill has finally found a publisher for the biography. It is a fairly specialised, small firm. Bill is offered its standard contract.

There is no advance but the royalties seem reasonable. Bill's concern is the cost of photographs and illustrations for the book. He finds it difficult to fund these 'up front'.

As Bill is a new author, the lack of advance may not necessarily be unreasonable. He must ensure he is not being asked for any subsidy himself (and is not involved with 'vanity press'). Bill should bear in mind the contract points listed in this chapter and also consider obtaining advice. He could, for example, join The Society of Authors as an associate member and have the contract vetted by them. He should explain his financial situation to the publisher and seek to negotiate a 'picture budget' to cover the costs of photographs and illustrations or at least obtain a contribution.

Daniel gets agented

After his problems with the TV company, Daniel decides that having an agent may strengthen his position. He has joined The Writers' Guild (traditionally more focused on drama, TV and radio and having special expertise regarding screenwriting). From them, he received recommendations as to a suitable agent who specialises in television work. The agent will take him on now that he is becoming fairly well-known, and is able to advise him on particular provisions required in any contract, such as repeat fees.

Daniel should ensure the agency contract is in writing. He should also consider obtaining legal advice before he commits himself. He should clarify whether the agency relates to all his work or just his television work. The agent then knows the basis of his commission. This aspect can cause friction if not made clear at the outset.

SUMMARY

• Always get an agreement recorded in writing.

• With magazines and newspapers, this will usually be through correspondence. Specify all main terms, such as publication, payment and date when this is due.

- If you obtain an agent, ensure the agency arrangements are noted in writing.

- With book publishers, a formal contract should be drawn up. In particular clarify royalties, the rights you are granting and the rights you retain.

- Seek advice/representation on specific terms. Possible sources include your agent, your solicitor, The Society of Authors and The Writers' Guild.

- Make sure you understand the terms before you sign. If necessary, ask for clarification and negotiate. Be polite, to the point and professional in such dealings.

DISCUSSION POINTS

1. Devise a letter to a magazine confirming a commission for an article, including points required to evidence a contract.

2. Set out, in order of priority, the realistic terms you would aim to agree in a book contract.

3. Consider which contract clauses you would strongly resist and what alternative compromises you might put forward to a publisher.

6
Getting Out of a Contract

I writ them a bill with mine own blood: the date is expired, this is the time, and he will fetch me.

(*Doctor Faustus*, Scene XIX, Christopher Marlowe)

WHAT IF IT ALL GOES WRONG?

Getting into a contract is easier than getting out of one. That is why it is important to ensure that the terms you agree to are ones which you can live with in the long term (see Chapter 5). That said, not even the crystal ball of a writer's imagination can foresee everything. An arrangement which suited you earlier may prove a millstone later. Therefore in this chapter you will look at potential 'get-outs'.

WHEN IS A CONTRACT NOT A CONTRACT?

The first possibility is to deny that a contract ever existed.

Certain **vitiating factors** can mean there never was true agreement. The contract is *void ab initio* (invalid from the beginning) or *voidable* (so that a party can elect to treat it as invalid).

Mistake
This is not a mistake in the ordinary sense. You might feel that a contract has been a big mistake. Perhaps it was not as profitable as you hoped. The law sees this as a mere mistake **as to quality**. To invalidate a contract the mistake has to be **fundamental**: for example, if you contracted to write a guidebook on Richmond, meaning the town in North Yorkshire, but the publisher intended Richmond-on-Thames.

Duress and undue influence
These apply where threat or coercion is used to make you enter a contract. The publisher may not literally hold a gun to your head, but what about metaphorically?

The modern concept of **economic duress** could be relevant. For this, there has to be more than just commercial pressure. Suppose, however, you complete a commissioned book but the publisher will only proceed if you agree to less advance and royalties. You point to the original terms, but the publisher gambles on your desperate need for immediate funds. You reluctantly agree to the new terms. In some circumstances it might be possible to argue later that the second agreement be overturned on grounds of economic duress (linked with lack of consideration – see Chapter 5).

Misrepresentation

This is where a person makes an **untrue statement of fact** to **induce** another to enter a contract.

This might apply, for example, where in certain circumstances a publisher grossly exaggerates to you the amount you will receive or the extent of promotion for your book. If you prove misrepresentation, you are usually entitled to **rescind** (undo) the contract and/or obtain damages.

HOW CAN I END MY CONTRACT?

The law recognises certain ways in which a contract may end. Some are amicable, some more hostile.

By agreement

No problem here. You and your agent or publisher (depending on the particular contract involved) agree to part company. This agreement is a new contract, superseding and releasing you both from the previous one.

By performance

Again no problem. You have fulfilled your part and your agent/ publisher has fulfilled theirs. The contract expires because its purpose is satisfied; for example a one-off commission for a set fee.

By frustration (or impossibility)

This occurs when **a contract is prevented** from being carried out, **not through the fault of either party**, but by an intervening event.

The event must be drastic enough to fundamentally change the circumstances **and** be something not contemplated at the time of the contract.

Sometimes a contract will include a *force majeure* clause giving a long list of intervening eventualities such as war or strike action. A short example, which aims to protect a writer, is:

'The Author shall not be liable for any failure in the performance of any of his/her obligations under this contract caused by factors outside his/her control.'

A commission to write a book is in effect a contract for personal service. You cannot subcontract to another author (unless you are a celebrity and ghost-writing is envisaged). If you cannot perform your obligations, because of, say, a **serious** accident, you could argue that the contract has been frustrated through personal incapacity, not that you are in breach because you cannot complete the work. This is supported by a 1960s case which held that, when the drummer of 'The Barron Knights' was too ill to perform, his contract was frustrated.

Example
You are commissioned to write a travelogue relating to a proposed visit to an Eastern European city. You find you cannot get there because of an outbreak of hostilities in the region. You might put forward a claim that the contract had therefore been frustrated. You could find you must return any advance, but may be allowed to deduct expenses properly incurred.

By breach

If you or the agent/publisher fail to carry out relevant obligations, on the face of it this is **breach of contract**. The innocent party can claim damages from the other (see later).

It matters whether the obligation breached amounts to an important term of the contract. This is legally classified as a **condition** rather than a **warranty** (a subsidiary provision – not to be confused with the same phrase meaning a type of guarantee). If there is a breach of condition, then the contract can be regarded as **discharged**. The innocent party can claim damages **and** treat the contract as at an end.

Terms likely to amount to conditions in a book contract are such as:

- on the publisher's part, the promise to publish and to pay royalties;

- on your part, the promise to complete a typescript and to correct proofs.

Provisions such as that the publisher will consult you on production

1. This contract shall terminate automatically if the Publisher convenes a meeting of its creditors or suffers a petition to be presented or other action to be taken with a view to its liquidation (other than for the purposes of and followed by amalgamation or reconstruction) or an administration order is made in relation to it or a receiver appointed over any of its property.

2. The Author may by thirty days written notice terminate this contract or suspend his/her performance of all or any of his/her obligations under it immediately and without liability for damages or other remedy if:

   a. the Publisher fails to comply with any of its obligations under this contract; or

   b. all editions of the work are out of print and the Publisher does not confirm its intention to reprint or reissue such work within thirty days of written request to do so by the author.

3. Upon termination, all rights in the work shall revert to the Author, but termination shall be without prejudice to any sub-licences properly granted by the Publisher or any claim or right of action already accrued to either party in respect of any breach of this contract by the other party.

Fig. 5. Sample termination clause.

hat you are entitled to free copies are likely to be considered warranties.

USING A TERMINATION CLAUSE

A termination clause in your contract could prove useful if things turn sour. It may also help you establish that rights in your work have reverted to you.

It can cover **automatic** termination on certain events (like the publisher going into liquidation). It may allow you to **give notice** to bring the contract to an end in particular circumstances. Keep a copy of any letter giving notice and send it by recorded delivery.

Figure 5 contains a sample termination clause to give you an idea of the events which might be covered in a contract with a publisher. Note that termination is stated at point 3 not to wipe out existing claims under the contract, for example, for outstanding royalties.

The exact clause suitable for your own contract depends on your circumstances. Additional points may be covered, such as a definition of 'out of print' agreed with your publisher.

GETTING REDRESS

Suppose the agent/publisher fails to fulfil contractual obligations? Probably the most frequent example is a publisher's refusal to publish your book – the publisher 'cancels the contract'. (This is colloquial, not legal terminology.) If this is not caused by your fault, you have fulfilled your side of the contract and assuming the publisher has no relevant 'get out' like an acceptance clause (see Chapter 5), what can you do?

Conciliation
Try to talk the situation through. Establish what the problem is. If a publisher has reservations about your typescript, for example, discuss possible changes. If the situation cannot be salvaged, discuss compensation. Generally, a negotiated out-of-court settlement is better for both parties. It avoids risk of losing, cost of litigation and unwelcome publicity.

If a compromise cannot be reached, you may have to consider your legal remedies. Even if the publisher makes an offer of settlement, you need to have some idea of the legal options to assess whether to accept, or to take your chances in court (see also Chapter 7).

Specific performance

This is an order compelling someone to perform their part of the contract. It is given at the court's discretion. Because it is an equitable remedy, certain maxims (principles) apply, including that you must have 'clean hands'. In other words, you must not be at fault in any way in the matter.

Damages

The courts award damages for breach of contract on the basis that you should be put in the same position **as if the contract was properly carried out**. This means that you should, in theory, receive compensation equal to the amount you would have received if the publisher had kept to the contract. This would include any unpaid advance and the royalties you were likely to earn, at least on the first print run.

You must, however, bear in mind that you are under a **duty to mitigate**. This means you have to do whatever you reasonably can to lessen your loss. You may have to show that you tried to find another publisher, or even improvise where appropriate such as by adapting a non-fiction work into articles. Any damages will be reduced accordingly.

One way to avoid a duty to mitigate can be to claim on a *quantum meruit* basis. This lawyer's Latin means basically that a fair sum should be paid for work done up to a certain point. You may be able to claim this where you are ready to fulfil your contractual obligations but the publisher in effect prevents you from doing so.

Example

In one case, an author was commissioned to write a volume on costume and ancient armour for a set fee payable on publication. He wrote part and would have completed the work, except for discovering that the publisher had ceased to publish the periodical for which the volume was required. The court awarded the writer half the set fee for work done so far. There was no onus on him to seek publication elsewhere.

CASE STUDIES

Liz fails the deadline

Liz has a commission in writing for a magazine feature on skiing in Scotland, where she is to visit an appropriate resort. This is required for a January issue by a strict copy date. Whilst practising on a local dry-ski slope, she suffers serious injury and is unable to travel or work at present.

Liz must inform the magazine as soon as possible. Her notification that she will be unable to deliver the feature for the deadline could be seen as **an anticipatory breach of contract** (a breach of obligation set to happen). She can argue instead that the contract has been frustrated because the intervening accident made it impossible for her to carry it out. If the magazine disputes this, she may need a doctor's statement. In any event, the magazine would be under a duty to mitigate its loss. It should be able to make alternative arrangements, given the present supply of freelance writers.

Bill the 'terminator'

Bill's publishers are dragging their heels even though it is nearly the centenary of the biographee's death. The contract states that publication is to be within eighteen months. The publishers assured him verbally when he signed, that they were keen to publish within six months. Bill is sceptical of the publishers bringing the book out. There is a termination clause in the contract.

Bill should take a firm stance. He should stress the eighteen-month period in the contract. He could even suggest misrepresentation as regards the verbal promises regarding six months. Bill can also point to the termination clause. Assuming it allows him to serve notice on breach of obligation by the publishers, he should make clear that he will not hesitate to do so – and claim damages. This may force the issue, but at least he will find out the publisher's true intention. His threats may make them think hard before 'cancelling'. Bill should stress the marketing opportunities which the centenary event could bring, to rekindle the publisher's enthusiasm.

Daniel ends a beautiful friendship

Daniel finds that he has a personality clash with his new agent. He has since been recommended to another agent, who has more expertise in his particular field.

Daniel should discuss the situation with the agent and point out that he feels that the relationship is not working. He should not have agreed to any attempt to make the agency irrevocable (see Chapter 5). If there is a termination clause in the agency contract, he should give written notice under this. The usual basis is that the agent will continue to receive any income due on deals he has previously arranged as Daniel's agent. It should be clarified whether the agent is to continue to sell rights in earlier work or whether all unsold work is to pass to the new agent.

SUMMARY

If you wish to end your contract:

* Consider whether any special factors could make it invalid, such as misrepresentation.

* Can it be ended by agreement, or has any unforeseen event intervened to frustrate the contract?

* If you have a termination clause in the contract, use it where applicable. Serve any notice by recorded delivery.

* Check whether the other party has failed to observe a condition so that you can treat the contract as discharged – and claim damages.

* Try to negotiate a solution where appropriate.

* If this is not possible, the legal remedy you are most likely to obtain for breach is damages.

* Such damages should be based on the amount you would have earned under the contract, subject to your duty to mitigate.

DISCUSSION POINTS

1. Which of the following could amount to misrepresentation:

   - a publisher, on picking up the signed contract which you have just placed on his desk, says, 'You won't regret this. You'll make a packet.'

   - a publisher, on handing to you the contract for signature, says 'No doubt you'll be giving up the day job. Twenty at least for you on the first print run.'

2. Taking the usual terms of a book contract (see Chapter 5), consider which may be important enough to be conditions, and which are likely to be only warranties.

3. Suppose a publisher 'cancels' a contract with you when you are a third of the way through the book and have incurred expenses of £100 in research. The advance agreed was £500. You estimate you would have received royalties of about £8,000. Think about the level of compensation for which you would press.

7
Getting Paid

No man but a blockhead ever wrote, except for money.
(Samuel Johnson, *Life of Johnson*, (J. Boswell) Vol. III.)

TAKING 'PERSUASIVE' MEASURES

You might feel that having sold your writing, you have done the hard part. Getting the money in can be even harder.

Many professional writers have 'cashflow difficulties'. Most are owed money by at least one publisher at any given time. The Freelance Network recently published a report highlighting this problem.

What can you do about it?

You must appreciate that as a mere writer, publishers regard you as a low priority when it comes to payment. The same applies to illustrators, photographers and models.

Publishers have a different attitude towards their commercial suppliers. Therefore it helps to project the right image – professional and businesslike, not disorganised and eccentric.

Think of yourself as a supplier of products (articles, stories, photographs, drawings, books) to your customer (the publisher).

Your 'credit control' steps

Below are some tips relating to articles, stories and other freelance items.

Before payment is due:

- Ensure any commission or acceptance is in writing (see Chapter 5).
- Send an invoice.

After payment is due:

- Send a reminder.
- Send another reminder seven days later.
- Telephone the accounts department.

- Telephone the editor.
- Send a letter before action.

Always keep a copy of everything.

The invoice

This should preferably be on a pre-printed invoice form or letter-headed paper.

It should be headed 'INVOICE' and include your name and address and those of the publisher, the name of the person who gave the commission/acceptance, a brief description of the work with any title, the sum owed, an invoice number, the present date and the due date for payment.

If no payment date has been agreed you could stipulate a date about one month after submission. If payment on publication is intended without any date set, you could insert:

'Payment due on publication or on or by (*insert a date about three months after submission*) whichever is the sooner'

Send your invoice to the publisher's **accounts department**. If the organisation is too small to have one, send it to the editor.

Reminders

The contents can be similar to those of the invoice but headed 'REMINDER' or 'ACCOUNT RENDERED' or 'STATEMENT'. Set up a standard on your PC, if possible.

Telephoning

This can keep the pressure up. A credit control theory suggests that a Monday morning call, though unpopular, is more effective. Remember the two 'P's – **politeness and persistence**.

One ploy can be to ask questions to which the answer is 'yes' or 'no'.

Example

– Did you receive my invoice?

– Do you agree this balance is due for payment?

– Will you send a cheque today?

If you are told 'the cheque's in the post', try asking when it was posted, whether first or second class and the cheque number.

Dear Sirs

Invoice number 0117

I refer to the above invoice in the sum of £150 which was submitted for your attention on 9 October.

Please note that unless payment is received by me within fourteen days of the date of this letter, court proceedings will be commenced against you without further notice. Such proceedings will include a claim for costs against you.

Yours faithfully

Fig. 6. Letter before action.

Letter before action

The action in question is court action. This letter should be fairly stern and precise – the last warning.

Such a letter is not a legal requirement, but if you sue without having sent one, you may not be able to reclaim court costs.

The letter should be on headed paper, be dated, refer to your invoice and when it was submitted, and state that, unless you receive payment within a specified time, you will initiate proceedings. Send it preferably by recorded delivery. Figure 6 gives an example.

You could instruct a solicitor in this. This will entail expense but, if you limit instructions to this preparatory step, not an inordinate amount. You could ask for a quote first. (Solicitors are under pressure from the Law Society to give accurate estimates.) Sometimes an organisation will pay by return of post as soon as it receives a solicitor's letter. It looks as though you mean business.

Another alternative is to instruct a debt collecting agency. They will charge for this service.

DECIDING TO SUE

You must take a commercial decision whether to sue or accept this unprofessional treatment for the sake of future goodwill.

As all lawyers stress, **there is no point in suing 'a man of straw'**. Look for signs whether the publication is in financial difficulties. Has it always paid promptly, but suddenly not now? Is the magazine issue coming out after its official publication date? Have many editorial staff recently left? If you suspect money trouble, it is a gamble to take further action. You could end up as another unsecured creditor, with a judgement with no assets to satisfy it.

Another factor to consider is the amount of the debt involved. If **£3,000 or below**, you should usually be able to use **the small claims court**. (Under the present Lord Chancellor's proposals, the financial limit is **likely to rise to £5,000** at some point in the future.) The expense is less and the procedure generally quicker and less formal. If a larger amount is involved, you may be embroiled in more complex and costly procedures, so think carefully.

USING THE SMALL CLAIMS COURT

This is a section of the county court. There is a county court in most towns. The procedure is not difficult and court offices are generally helpful to **litigants in person** (people not represented by a solicitor). You can sort out specific queries with them.

For general guidance, the normal steps are:

• Send a **letter before action**.

• If you are still unpaid after the time specified in that letter, obtain the forms mentioned below from the court office, with accompanying notes and explanatory booklet.

• Complete a **default summons** (form N1) in triplicate. This can be in hand or typed. Insert your full name and address (as **plaintiff**) together with those of the publisher (the **defendant**) and the amount owed.

• In the box headed '**Particulars of Claim**' give details of the debt. An example is given in Figure 7.

• Return these to court with the appropriate fee, usually between £10 and £70, depending on the amount claimed. Cheques should be payable to 'H M Paymaster General'. If you can show hardship, ask the court office for a fee exemption/reduction.

• Add any fee to the total claimed in your summons.

> The Plaintiff claims the sum of one hundred and fifty pounds (£150) being the amount due under an invoice dated 31 March 199X and owed by the Defendant in respect of a story entitled *No Regrets*, written by the Plaintiff. The said story was sold to the Defendant on 1 February 199X and published by the Defendant in April 199X.

Fig. 7. Sample particulars of claim.

• The court will issue the summons. If there is no reply within the court's fourteen-day limit, complete form N205A requesting **judgement in default**.

Once you have judgement, you can **enforce** this through court methods, such as bailiffs, if necessary. It is unlikely that matters will come to this. Most organisations reach for the cheque book upon receiving the summons. They are usually anxious to avoid a judgement registered against them, which could affect their credit rating.

If there is any **dispute**, such as over the exact amount owed, there will usually be an **arbitration** hearing before the District Judge. This is fairly informal. You should attend but do not have to have a solicitor. Take your relevant copy documents as evidence.

A dispute can sometimes lead to the case being transferred to a court more convenient to the defendant. In general, though, the administrative time involved makes it unlikely that any organisation would defend in a clear-cut debt case.

What about book publishers?

Your contract should specify payment dates for royalties. Often it is twice a year on set dates. Diarise these. If payment does not arrive around this time, get in touch with any agent who negotiated the contract or telephone the publishers' accounts department. Again politeness and persistence pays.

CLAIMING FOR LARGER AMOUNTS

Debt recovery for freelance items usually falls within the financial limits of the small claims court. Most larger amounts are recovered through the county court, with very large or complex cases often heard in the High Court.

The procedure there is more formal and complicated. It is not within the scope of this book to describe this in depth. You can bring your case without legal representation and the court offices are generally helpful. It is, however, more difficult. Also bear in mind that, unlike in the small claims court, if you lose, you could have to pay the other side's legal costs.

You could consider consulting a solicitor. Ask about **legal aid**. The limits for eligibility have narrowed in recent years, but you may qualify for some help. The catch is that if you win, you may have to refund your legal aid from anything recovered.

Some solicitors now conduct cases on a 'no win, no fee' basis, similar to that in the USA.

REACHING A SETTLEMENT

Most disputes never reach the courtroom. The power of your legal rights often lies more in their potential than in actual litigation.

In straightforward debt cases, the only settlement you should consider is payment in full. Where there is dispute, such as over the amount of fee agreed, and you have no conclusive evidence on your side, consider any reasonable offer put to you. Make no admission as to any fault yourself.

Generally it is better to negotiate over the telephone or face to face, rather than through correspondence. If possible, let the other side mention a figure first. If it is derisory, reject it. Otherwise, say you will get back to them, rather than make an impulsive decision. If you have incurred expense, like a summons fee, ensure this is included in any amount you agree.

Any written offer will probably be headed 'without prejudice'. You would be wise to head your own correspondence with this when negotiating. It will usually be implied in oral negotiations too, but it is just as well to make this clear before you start discussions. This phrase basically means that if you reject the offer, you cannot later refer to it in court to prove an admission of fault. Once you accept the offer, the correspondence loses this 'privilege'. It can be used to prove the agreement for payment to you of the amount offered. You have then reached a settlement.

CASE STUDIES

Liz takes action
A magazine to which Liz has supplied stories regularly has not paid

her for the last two. Both were accepted in writing with payment to be on publication, and have now been published.

Liz has already invoiced and followed through the procedure of reminders and telephone chasers to the accounts department. She has sent a 'letter before action'. The silence is still deafening. Being reasonably confident that the magazine is solvent, she now issues proceedings in the small claims court. The magazine sends her a cheque for the debt. She telephones them to make clear that the summons fee is also part of her claim. They send this in the next post.

Bill inspects

The biography has now been published. Sales are modest, but, partly due to local publicity, are at a reasonable level. Bill, however, has not received any royalties.

Bill checks the payment provisions in his contract and the publishers' royalty accounting periods. Payment is clearly in arrears. He contacts the publishers' accounts department to enquire whether there has been an 'oversight'. He is told they will look into it. He still receives nothing. He writes a polite letter giving notice of his intention to exercise his right to inspect the accounts so far as they relate to his book. He quotes the relevant clause in the contract containing this right, and suggests a date and time. The accounts department seem to resent this potential intrusion. A cheque and statement arrive a few days later.

Daniel settles out of court

The TV company for whom Daniel has been working wishes to bring in a new writer for the next series of the sit-com. Daniel is not too perturbed because he wants to pursue other work. His new agent has 'irons in the fire' on this. The agent had insisted that he received a written contract for the present series. Under it the TV company cannot terminate just yet.

Daniel opens negotiations for compensation through his agent. The agent recommends a media solicitor be consulted. The solicitor issues proceedings, to put pressure on the TV company.

'Without prejudice' negotiations take place and an offer is made. Daniel is advised to reject this as insufficient. The TV company makes a 'payment into court' of this amount. This is a tactic often used by a defendant. It has the effect that if the case proceeds to trial and the judge awards less or equal to the offer, then the plaintiff usually has to pay some of the other side's costs. It places Daniel under pressure to reach a settlement. Negotiations continue. The agent and solicitor advise Daniel on a reasonable sum to accept. The TV company offer almost this amount. Daniel decides to take the 'bird in the hand'. This settlement is recorded in writing. The solicitor also arranges for it to be embodied in a court order to ensure there is prompt payment.

SUMMARY

- For articles, stories and similar freelance items, chase up payment through:
  - invoicing
  - reminders
  - telephone enquiries
  - a letter before action
  - the small claims court.

- For book publishers, diarise contractual dates and contact the publishers' accounts department as soon as you realise that payment is overdue.

- Use threats of legal action to speed up payment and to negotiate a settlement in any dispute.

- Only sue if you believe your defendant to be solvent.

- Use the small claims court if the debt is within its financial limits.

- With larger debts, consider taking legal advice. Beware of the risk of costs being awarded against you if you lose.

ACTION POINTS

1. Devise a standard invoice and reminder letter, preferably on PC, to use when need arises.

2. Contact your local county court for the appropriate leaflets and forms regarding small claims, so that you have these to hand.

3. Draft a standard letter before action. Keep this as your 'precedent' to use if necessary.

8
Sorting Out Other Problems

He that handleth a matter wisely shall find good.

(Proverbs, Chapter 16 verse 20)

This chapter comprises questions on common problems you may encounter, together with possible solutions.

How long can they sit on it?

You might ask this when selling articles or stories to a magazine, or when you have a manuscript with an agent or a book under consideration with a publisher.

There are few legal strictures to help you, unless you get a time expressly agreed. You can insert a limit as a device to 'encourage' editors not to keep you waiting. For example, one freelance, a former journalist with a national newspaper, inserts 'on offer for publication within two months' at the top of copy.

A good agent should give you progress reports, not fobbing-off with vague references to your work being with a publisher. The agent is acting for you after all. Find out which publishing houses have considered the manuscript and brief details of their reactions.

If a publisher takes months to respond to you, consider chasing this up diplomatically in writing or by telephone. Some publishers, such as Headline, giving warning on receipt of submissions if substantial delay is likely. If you are established on the publisher's list, press your editor when delay becomes unreasonable. You could possibly complain to their senior person if delay becomes inordinate.

What if my material is edited without permission?

On a pragmatic basis, it is generally accepted that some editing is required to suit commercial needs. Editors usually aim to improve grammar and abbreviate when necessary. House style is relevant. Most writers welcome such assistance.

If your whole self-expression and meaning has been distorted, your moral rights (see Chapter 2) may come into play. You may be able to insist on amendment, obtain an apology or publicly disassociate yourself from the change, depending on exact circumstances.

Can I charge a 'kill-fee'?

Some freelances have made effective demands for a 'kill-fee'. One found that mention of this stopped an editor trying to back-track on a commissioned work. 'Kill-fee' is not a legal term, nor an automatic right. A few magazines pay for abortive work as their normal practice. Otherwise you may have to show a 'kill-fee' was agreed in the contract. Be careful not to insert anything too excessive which might become a form of penalty clause, as these are technically void in law. 'Agreed damages clauses' are allowed for realistic compensation agreed in advance. Therefore, any fee stated should be a genuine estimate of your loss through cancellation. Fifty per cent of the full fee is paid by some publications and this may be a good amount for which to aim.

I have described myself in my writer's CV as a contributor to certain magazines. Do I need their permission?

Very unlikely. That said, any statement must be correct and not misleading.

A corporation has annexed a large chunk from a textbook I produced and annexed copies of it to its staff manual. Is this allowed?

Almost certainly not. The *de minimus* rule and fair dealing (see Chapter 3) are unlikely to apply. Unless your publisher has some special agreement with the company you should ask him to take up this matter, possibly through the CLA (see Chapter 3).

9
Appreciating Legal Aspects
of Self-Publishing

I find more and more that my style of Designing is a Species by
itself... resolv'd to shew an independence which I know will please an
Author.

(*Letter to the Reverend Dr Trusler*, William Blake)

IS IT FOR YOU?

If you are grappling with this question, you are in good company.
Virginia Woolf, Beatrix Potter and John Galsworthy are just a few
past pens who did so. More recently, Timothy Mo and Jill Paton
Walsh (both short-listed for the Booker Prize) took this step.

Self-publishing is thriving amongst many quality authors. An
Author–Publisher Network exists to provide a forum (address at the
back of this book). For many fiction writers, self-publishing offers
an alternative to unfavourable slush-pile odds and the stigma of
vanity publishing. Non-fiction writers often feel they know their
market better than any publisher.

Therefore assuming your answer is 'yes', several of the legal
implications to bear in mind are discussed in this chapter.

CHOOSING THE TYPE OF ORGANISATION

As in any business venture, there is the issue of what form – or 'legal
personality' – to take. Alternatives to operating as an individual
include a **partnership**, a **limited company** or **an association such as a
club**.

If you are effectively a 'one man band'/sole trader, you may be
happy to carry on by yourself. If pooling resources with someone
else, perhaps your spouse or a group of committed friends, you may
become a partnership. The Partnership Act says this is:

'the relation which subsists between persons carrying on a
business in common with a view of profit'

You do not have to make a profit – only operate to achieve it. Nor do you need a written partnership agreement, although in some circumstances (especially if partners are contributing money in unequal shares) it is a good idea to have one drawn up.

The maximum number of partners usually allowed is twenty. Over this, you must become a company.

FORMING A COMPANY OR CLUB

In deciding whether to become a company, you may need professional advice. One consideration is the limited liability which this brings. This means that, as a general rule, you cannot personally be sued for any debts (unlike in a partnership). This could to some extent guard you from large libel or copyright infringement claims. Sometimes insurance can be obtained, such as through Sun Alliance Financial Risks Ltd (see addresses at the back of this book). One group debated this choice but eventually opted to become a club to avoid some expense and formality.

Clubs can take various forms. They can be simply an association of individuals who share a common purpose (such as the furtherance of writing), with a relatively informal constitution. At the other end of the spectrum, they can be an incorporated entity, normally registered as a 'company limited by guarantee', needing no share capital and limiting members' liability to a certain amount.

Companies have a constitution set out in a **Memorandum of Association**. This includes an objects clause (see below) and articles. Articles are rules to regulate the internal organisation, such as for meetings and company resolutions. A standard format called Table A may be adopted.

Objects clause

This states the objectives the company will have. It is important because technically the company can only act within such objectives. It is often lengthy, with subsections listing subsidiary aims and powers, such as the borrowing of money. Sometimes these include or are replaced by a simple statement that the company shall carry on business as a general commercial company (under section 110 of the Companies Act 1989). There is usually a main objects clause, which encapsulates the primary aims.

A sample is set out in Figure 8. This involves a fictional company formed by two imaginary former partners, John Butler and Melanie Clark, who now require limited liability.

Memorandum of Association of Butler and Clark Publishing Enterprises Limited

1. The name of the Company is Butler and Clark Publishing Enterprises Limited.

2. The registered office of the Company will be situated in England and Wales.

3. The objects for which the Company is established are:

    a. To carry on the business of self-publishers, including the publishing, selling, marketing and promotion of all types of books, magazines, leaflets and other literature, whether fiction or non-fiction.

    b. To carry on business as a general commercial company.

    c. To carry on any other business whatsoever which in the opinion of the Board of Directors is connected with or ancillary to the main business of the company as stated above.

Fig. 8. Sample extract of a Memorandum of Association, including the main objects clause.

Bearing in mind the tax position

Tax aspects are important because, depending upon your personal circumstances, one form may be more advantageous than another. You would therefore need to seek your accountant's advice over this.

CHOOSING A NAME

You will probably adopt a business name to represent your imprint and give additional credibility. You may find that your bank insists upon this when opening an account for your venture.

Avoid any name already in use or very similar to an existing name because of the risk of 'passing-off' (see Chapter 2) or anything misleading. Check for example with the Companies Registration Office (Tel: 01222 388588) and in writers' handbooks.

Remember that the Business Names Act requires your real name to appear on general stationery, receipts and invoices.

DEALING WITH OTHER FORMALITIES

International Standard Book Numbers

ISBNs are ten-digit reference numbers printed on a book's jacket and the verso (reverse/left-hand side) of any title page. They identify country of origin, publisher and the work concerned, and are allocated to books for sale by retail.

You can obtain the numbers free of charge for books you intend to publish from the ISBN Agency at Whitaker & Sons Ltd. (see addresses at the back of this book).

An ISBN enables your book to be easily identified and traced by booksellers and potential readers. Chains such as W. H. Smith will not stock work without one. As some are now buying from self-publishers, why risk losing this chance for the sake of a technicality?

Book listing

Whitakers also list your titles in certain useful directories. Complete and return their **yellow form** three months in advance of publication.

Your titles will be included in a list in *The Bookseller* which can result in sales. Nik Morton of Morton Publishing, Gosport, self-published a niche crime novel and through listing received an order from London's Murder One crime bookshop. Sometimes titles appear in directories such as *British Books in Print, Books of the Month* and *Children's Books in Print.*

Beware some of the mailshots you may receive as a result of listing, such as from printers and bookbinders. Money-saving offers on volume may leave you with too many books to sell.

British Library Cataloguing-in-Publication Data Programme
This is administered by the British Library. Complete the appropriate form, obtainable from the British Library (see addresses at the back of this book).

Depositing copies with Libraries
Under the Copyright Act of 1911 (since modified), publishers were placed under a duty to deposit a copy of any title, within one month of publication with the British Library and, if requested, the following:

- The Bodleian Library, Oxford
- The Library of Cambridge University
- The Library of Trinity College, Dublin
- The National Library of Scotland
- The National Library of Wales

You can send the British Library copy direct, and the others care of Mr A. T. Smail, the Agent for the Copyright Libraries (see addresses at the back of this book).

Advertising
A crucial aspect of self-publishing is marketing. Without a good strategy, your books may remain unsold.

Advertising methods include flyers, press releases, blurbs and hype of any description – but remember there are codes of advertising and sales promotion. The first principle of **The Advertising Code** is that:

'all advertisements should be legal, decent, honest and truthful.'

You can obtain free advice on your advertising and promotions regarding the regulations from the Advertising Standards Authority (see addresses at the back of this book).

Assert your moral right
Don't forget that your right to be properly accredited as author must be asserted in writing (see Chapter 2). Usually you cover this in any publishing contract you enter. As self-publisher you are in

control of this. Insert an assertion on the verso of the title page. (See example given in Chapter 2.)

Book-keeping and tax

Even if your self-publishing income is fairly low to start with, keep at least a cash book listing all your incomings and outgoings as they occur.

Provided you operate as a business to make a profit, you can normally claim any expenses against tax. Consult your accountant as necessary on the finer details.

Registering for VAT

You may find this unnecessary. The registration threshold from 29 November 1995 is, in broad terms, set at an annual turnover of £47,000. If you are likely to reach this, seek advice; for example, from your accountant or by ringing your local Customs and Excise Department.

If you are eligible to register, you may be able to reclaim any VAT charged (or inputted) to you; for example, VAT on printing costs.

CASE STUDIES

Liz gets an offer

Liz is dismayed at the trouble in placing her latest novel, which she has completed after a year's hard work. It is more experimental than her previous work.

She is cheered by a win in a national short story competition. As a result, she gives an interview on local radio, discussing her work in general. She later receives a letter purporting to offer to publish her novel. After the rejections she has received, she is tempted by 'the chance to see your work in print at a fair price' stated in the letter.

Liz has almost certainly been mailshotted by a subsidy publisher, who perhaps obtained her name and address after hearing the interview. She would be well-advised to look beyond any enticing statements in initial correspondence.

The Advertising Standards Authority recently concluded research into advertising practices of the 'vanity press'. The main concern was that advertisers might mislead clients on promotion intended for each book and the potential profits. The Authority has written a new *Advice Note* directed at such publishers.

That is not to say that there are not some reputable subsidy publishers who can offer a worthwhile service.

It is doubtful, however, whether this is something for Liz. She could persevere with trying to find another publisher. Alternatively she could opt for self-publishing; for example, using desk-top facilities. The initial outlay may not be cheap, though prices of systems fluctuate like all new technology and dealers will negotiate. It may represent a better investment for her than contributing to subsidy publishing, and this way she will be in control.

Bill the poet

Several of Bill's poems have been accepted in fairly respectable small press literary publications, but he cannot find any publisher who will bring out a volume.

The market for poetry is limited. This has made some poets particularly susceptible to misleading claims of less scrupulous vanity publishers, as highlighted by Johnathon Clifford of the National Poetry Foundation.

Bill may find self-publishing is a suitable option. Poetry is difficult to sell, but he may have a sufficiently wide circle of friends or contacts who will subscribe. He may intend local distribution only. He will probably not wish to invest in desk-top equipment. He could consider contracting-out the printing. Most reputable printers will do short runs. He could also set his material on disc, passing it on to a specialist firm to typeset and continue to full book finishing. Technical services of this nature can be found through the trade press. Bill should obtain written quotes and stipulate a deadline for completion of the work.

Daniel and the anthology

Daniel belongs to a county playwrights' group. With so few plays published, members decide to collaborate on producing an anthology of their works.

One of the main decisions to be taken is the amount each will contribute to the venture. They need to produce an estimate of the expense to ascertain this. If they intend to sell the anthology at a profit, they may decide to operate as a partnership. It would be advisable to have a written agreement to record the respective contributions and other terms agreed. Provision should be included for how the partnership can be dissolved (brought to an end).

SUMMARY

• Decide if self-publishing is a good move for your particular writing career.

- If so, there are technicalities to note – but not to deter you.

- Decide on how you will operate and the form of business you wish to take. Take professional advice as necessary.

- Choose a business name for your imprint. Ensure this is not too similar to an existing name and is not misleading.

- Bear in mind formalities, such as ISBN, book listing, library copies, advertising regulations and assertion of your moral rights.

- Consult your accountant as necessary regarding book-keeping and tax, particularly VAT if applicable.

DISCUSSION POINTS

1. Consider which form of business venture you would be most likely to take as a self-publisher.

2. A self-publisher must be 'hands on' as regards book production. List the types of formalities you would have to bear in mind as a self-publisher, which would not concern you as simply an author.

3. Which kind of titles do you feel would be especially suited to self-publishing?

10
Dealing With Your Literary Estate

So long as men can breathe or eyes can see
So long lives this and this gives life to thee.

(Sonnet XVIII, Shakespeare)

MAKING A WILL

In making a will, it is advisable to consult a professional. Lawyers often remark that they make more money out of 'home-made' wills than those they draft themselves, due to disputes which can later arise over defects. Many solicitors charge a relatively modest fee (often in the hope that if the will remains lodged with them, they will have a chance of later getting the job of administering the estate).

All authors should take into account their literary estate when making a will. If published, you may require a particular person to inherit royalties. Even if unpublished, you may wish to leave your work in the hands of someone likely to safeguard it.

You can bequeath (give in your will) an original manuscript. It is implied with an unpublished manuscript that copyright of the work passes with it. Alternatively, you can specify to whom copyright/the right to receive royalties is to go. Your moral rights (see Chapter 2) usually pass to the person inheriting the copyright but you can nominate someone else to take these over. The paternity and integrity rights last as long as the copyright. The right against false attribution expires twenty years after your death.

CHOOSING THE RIGHT EXECUTORS

Executors carry out the will. The beneficiaries inherit under it. They can be one and the same, or different people.

Executors and beneficiaries named in respect of your general property may not be your preference to entrust with your writings. The same applies if you name no executors, or die intestate (without a will), in which case your next of kin under the intestacy rules take over. It is better to make express provision.

If you have an agent, he/she may be the obvious choice to take over your literary estate. The term 'literary executor' is not a legal one but will probably be used by the agent. You may appoint the agent to be in effect a trustee of your literary assets for the benefit of named beneficiaries. Alternatively, you could just request that the 'literary executor' advise the main executors regarding your literary assets.

If you are unpublished, you may prefer writer-friends to take charge of your works, or persons to whom you feel they were indirectly dedicated. Your autobiography may, for example, be important to your grandchildren.

PLANNING FOR THE FUTURE

Legal problems can arise in leaving money to promote your work after your death. The law will not usually allow a trust set up indefinitely for a purpose, rather than to benefit a group or an individual. Exceptions exist, such as for charities, and there are ways round the matter. One alternative is to leave money to a friend and express a hope that they will use it for the purpose you require. This area is, however, in general hedged with many technical rules, making specialist legal drafting advisable.

You could leave the right to royalties or a lump sum to a relevant charity; for example, the Royal Literary Fund or the Theatres Trust.

TAX

The Capital Taxes Office is not usually unreasonable when it comes to agreeing probate valuations of literary estates. Estimates by your publisher or agent will be relevant. Inheritance tax must be borne in mind when your will is drafted. You may need professional advice on minimising tax, perhaps by lifetime transfers or appropriate provision in your will.

CASE STUDIES

Each of the three writers you have followed through the case studies would consider their position regarding their respective literary estates according to their own particular circumstances. A brief overview of the possibilities is considered below.

Liz

Liz's executor for her general estate will probably be her husband. She may be happy for him also to administer her literary matters – particularly if he is the sole beneficiary under her will, and is therefore to receive royalties from her work.

Bill

Bill may wish to nominate a writer-friend to take control of his literary estate, or perhaps a relative who has encouraged him in his writing.

Daniel

Daniel would doubtless appoint his agent as 'literary executor'. He should ensure that the agent is given full control in copyright matters, so that any infringement can be properly challenged and Daniel's work fully safeguarded.

SUMMARY

- It is advisable to have your will professionally drawn up.

- Give careful consideration to whom you name as suitable to take over your literary estate.

- Specialist drafting may be required if you wish to give directions on the future promotion of your work.

DISCUSSION POINTS

1. Why do you think it is important that an author's work is left in safe hands?

2. Consider why it may be advisable to appoint a specific 'literary executor'.

3. What do you feel are the characteristics which a good 'literary executor' should have?

Glossary

Acknowledgement. Written credit to the author of a source used.

Case law. Body of legal precedents, comprising decisions in previous cases.

Contract. A legally binding agreement.

Copyright. In general terms, the right over use of original literary, musical, dramatic or artistic works.

Damages. Compensation awarded by the civil courts.

Data Protection. Regulations over the holding of information about people on computer.

Defamation. A tort concerning injury to reputation through such things as untrue statements.

Directives. A form of European legislation.

Equity. A body of English law based upon equitable principles of fairness.

Estoppel. A legal doctrine which can sometimes prevent someone denying a previous statement or going back on a promise.

Fair dealing. An exception to usual copyright restrictions.

Injunction. A court order to prevent, or sometimes compel, certain action.

Intellectual property. The body of law concerned with matters like copyright, trademarks, patents and passing-off.

Law. References in this book are generally to **the law of England and Wales** and as it applies mainly to British persons.

Legislation. Laws embodied in forms such as Acts of Parliament or statutory instruments.

Libel. Defamation in a permanent form.

Licence. A permission, usually in writing, for a certain act.

Litigation. Disputes involving court proceedings.

Magistrates. Justices of the peace, who are usually lay persons, not legally qualified, who hear criminal cases in the magistrates courts.

Moral rights. Legal rights associated with copyright and aimed at protecting reputation.

Passing-off. A tort concerning a claim that someone has wrongly represented goods or work as being associated with someone else.

Patent. Legal means of protecting an invention from use by another.

Plagiarism. A pejorative term for using someone else's work.

Public domain. When a work is no longer protected by copyright.

Slander. In broad terms, defamation in a verbal form.

Tort. A civil wrong for which an individual can sue in the civil courts.

Trade mark. An identification symbol, slogan or other marketing device or sign.

Trading Standards Departments. Local departments which enforce legislation such as The Trade Descriptions Act and can help consumers against unscrupulous commercial practices.

Trust. The legal means by which property or money is held by a trustee for the benefit of another (the beneficiary).

Typographical arrangement. The arrangement of printed words.

Will. A legal document which enforces the wishes of a person after their death in relation to their property.

Useful Addresses

The Advertising Standards Authority, 2 Torrington Place, London WC1E 7HW. Tel: (0171) 580 4100.

The Agent for the Copyright Libraries (Mr A. T. Smail), 100 Euston Street, London NW1 2HQ. Tel: (0171) 388 5061.

The British Library, Legal Deposit Office, Boston Spa, Wetherby LS23 7BQ.

The Copyright Licensing Agency, 90 Tottenham Court Road, London W1P OLP. Tel: (0171) 436 5931.

Catalyst Media, Studio A, 6 Corfton Road, Ealing, London W5 2HS.

Sun Alliance Financial Risks Ltd, 1 Leadenhall Street, London EC3V 1PP. Tel: (0171) 588 2345.

The Author–Publisher Network, c/o 7 Kingsland Road, West Mersea, Essex CO5 8RB.

The British Copyright Council, Copyright House, 29–39 Berner Street, London W1P 4AA. Tel: (0171) 359 1895.

The Data Protection Registrar, Wycliffe House, Water Lane, Wilmslow, Cheshire SK9 5AF. Tel: (01625) 545745.

The Intellectual Property Policy Directorate of the Patent Office, Hazlitt House, 45 Southampton Buildings, London WC2A 1AR. Tel: (0171) 438 4777.

The ISBN Agency, Whitaker & Sons Ltd, 12 Dyott Street, London WC1A 1DF. Tel: (0171) 836 8911.

The National Union of Journalists, Acorn House, 314 Gray's Inn Road, London WC1X 8DP. Tel: (0171) 278 7916.

The Public Lending Right Office, Bayheath House, Prince Regent Street, Stockton-on-Tees, Cleveland, TS18 1DF. Tel: (01642) 604699.

The Society of Authors, 84 Drayton Gardens, London SW10 9SB. Tel: (0171) 373 6642.

The Society of Women Writers and Journalists, c/o 110 Whitehall Road, Chingford, London E4 6DW.

The Writers' Guild of Great Britain, 430 Edgware Road, London
W2 1EH. Tel: (0171) 723 8074.

The Women's Writers Network, c/o 23 Prospect Road, London
NW2 2JU.

Further Reading

Intellectual Property, David I. Bainbridge, 2nd edition, Pitman Publishing, 1994.

McNae's Essential Law for Journalists, Tom Welsh and Walter Grenwood, 13th edition, Butterworths, 1995.

Smith and Keenan's Advanced Business Law, Denis Keenan, 8th edition, Pitman Publishing, 1992.

Drafting Settlements of Disputes, Michael Arnheim, Tolley Publishing Company Limited, 1994.

An Author's Guide to Publishing, Michael Legat, Robert Hale, 1994.

Vanity Press and the Proper Poetry Publishers, Johnathon Clifford, ISBN 0 95225035 7.

How to Publish a Book, Robert Spicer, How To Books Ltd, ISBN 1 85703 161 X.

How to Do Your Own Advertising, Michael Bennie, How To Books Ltd, ISBN 1 85703 213 6.

Media Law, G. Robertson QC and A. Nicoll, 2nd edition, Longman.

International Standard Book Numbering, 7th edition, The Standard Book Numbering Agency Ltd, 1993.

The Cassell Handbook of Copyright in British Publishing Practice, 3rd edition, 1993 ISBN 0 30432635 6.

How to Publish a Newsletter, Graham Jones, How To Books Ltd, ISBN 1 85703 166 0.

Making a Complaint, Helen Shay, How To Books Ltd. ISBN 1 85703 102 4.

How to Write for Publication, Chriss McCallum, How To Books Ltd, ISBN 1 85703 140 7.

Index

acceptance, 46, 56
account of profits, 17
accounts, 50, 51, 74
acknowledgements, 28–7, 31
adaptations, 20, 22, 25–6
advance, 50, 51
advertising, 82
Advertising Standards Authority, 82, 91
agents, 48–9, 57, 76
anthologies, 30, 54, 84
apology, 43, 44
assignment of copyright, 51–2
Author–Publisher Network, 78, 91

Berne Convention, 16, 18, 21
bibliographies, 31
biography, 25, 44
book-keeping, 83
book listing, 81
breach of contract, 62–5
British Library, 82, 91
business names, 81

capacity, 47
CD-rom, 53
civil proceedings, 17, 18, 38, 71–3
clubs, 78–9
commissions, 48, 49, 68
common knowledge, 29, 31
companies, 78–80
compensation, 17, 63–4
conciliation, 63, 73
confidence, law of, 12, 32–3
consensus ad idem, 47

consideration, 46, 60
contract, 12, 16, 46–67
conventions, 19, 21
copyright, 11, 16–37, 51–4, 86
Copyright, Designs and Patents Act 1988, 19, 21–7
Copyright Licensing Agency, 34, 53, 77, 91
copyright notice, 19, 26, 27
county court, 71–3
courts, 17, 38, 71–3
criminal offences, 17, 38
criticism, 30, 43

damages, 17, 64
data protection, 34–5
debt collecting, 12
defamation, 38–45
default summons, 71
defences, 19, 24, 42
de minimus, 29, 77
drama, 26, 44–5
duration of copyright, 17–18, 24, 25
duress, 59–60

economic duress, 60
electronic rights, 52–3
e-mail, 39
equitable principles, 32
estoppel, 23
European legislation, 18, 53
executors, 86–7

fair dealing, 30, 34
false attribution, 22–3

film rights, 52
first serial rights, 54
force majeure, 60–1
frustration, 60–1

illustrations, 57
impossibility, 60–1
injunction, 17, 39
injurious falsehood, 40
innocent infringement, 19, 24
innuendo, 40
integrity right, 22–4, 76–7
Internet, 53
invoice, 68–70
ISBN, 81

juries, 38
justification, 42

Legal Aid, 38, 73
legal costs, 73
legality, 47
letter before action, 70
libel, 12, 38–45
licensing of copyright, 12, 51–2
literary estates, 86–8

magazines, 46–8, 55
magistrates, 17
malice, 43
minimum terms agreement, 50
misrepresentation, 47, 60
mistake, 59
mitigation, 64
moral rights, 12, 19, 21–7, 82

National Poetry Foundation, 84
negotiating, 55, 73

objections, 22–3
options, 56

particulars of claim, 71–2
partnerships, 78–9
passing-off, 29, 81
patent, 16

paternity right, 22–4, 26, 51
payment into court, 74
pen names, 23, 29
permissions, 36, 77
photocopying, 34
piracy, 17, 53
plagiarism, 12, 31–4
plays, 26, 44–5
poetry, 30, 84
presentation, 28
privity of contract, 47

quantum meruit, 64
quoting, 13, 29–30

radio, 26, 52
remaindering, 56
reminders, 68–9
royalties, 50, 51, 72

second serial rights, 54
self-publishing, 78–85
settlement, 73–5
slander, 12, 38
small claims court, 71–2, 74
Society of Authors, 30, 55, 91
solicitors, 71, 55
sources, 28–37, 42
subconscious copying, 33–4
sub-licences, 50, 52
substantial part, 29–30

tax, 81, 87
television, 36, 52
termination clauses, 49, 62–3, 65
titles, 29, 50
tort, 32, 38
trademarks, 16, 29
Trading Standards Department, 17
translations, 52
trusts, 12, 32, 87
typographical arrangements, 24

uncertainty, 47
US rights, 52

VAT, 83
vanity press, 57, 83
vitiating factors, 59–60

waiver, 23
warranty, 56, 61

wills, 12, 13, 86–8
without prejudice, 73, 74
Writers' Guild, 55
writers' workshops and circles, 24, 84